CUNARD

QUEEN MARY 2

PHILIP DAWSON

Published by: Ferry Publications, PO Box 33, Ramsey, Isle of Man IM99 4LP

Tel: +44 (0) 1624 898445   Fax: +44 (0) 1624 898449   E-mail: ferrypubs@manx.net   Website: www.ferrypubs.co.uk

Published by:
Ferry Publications, PO Box 33, Ramsey, Isle of Man IM99 4LP
Tel: +44 (0) 1624 898445   Fax: +44 (0) 1624 898449
E-mail: ferrypubs@manx.net   Website: www.ferrypubs.co.uk

CONTENTS

Produced and designed by Ferry Publications trading as Lily Publications Ltd

PO Box 33, Ramsey, Isle of Man, British Isles, IM99 4LP

Tel: +44 (0) 1624 898446   Fax: +44 (0) 1624 898449

www.ferrypubs.co.uk   E-Mail: info@lilypublications.co.uk

Printed and bound by 1010 Printing, China © Lily Publications 2011

Second Edition: September 2013 Third Edition: November 2014

*Aglow at dusk on a late autumn evening in Normandy, the brand new **Queen Mary 2** lies alongside at the Chantiers de l'Atlantique shipyard, the overhead crane swung back from above her decks in readiness for her imminent handover to the Cunard Line. (Chantiers de l'Atlantique)*

4

INTRODUCTION

With this work we complete our trilogy of the 21st century Cunard Line 'Queens' 'Victoria' and 'Elizabeth' with the addition here of the Line's current flagship, the *Queen Mary 2*. When the first *Queen Mary* and *Queen Elizabeth* passed each other at speed for the very last time at night during September 1967 in the North Atlantic service that was their lifeblood, it was said that the likes of such great ships were probably never going to be seen again. While this was true insofar as the old 'Queens' belonged to a bygone era, these much-loved liners were in other regards nonetheless already influencing the new dual purpose North Atlantic and cruising *Queen Elizabeth 2* completed in 1969. No doubt even more remarkably, the legacy of the original 'Queens' was also to shape some aspects of the following-generation *Queen Mary 2* and her two 'Queen'-class fleet mates the *Queen Victoria* and *Queen Elizabeth* more than 40 years later – and so it is that the Cunard Line enters its illustrious third century of service with, for the first time in its history, three 'Queens'.

The history of sustained North Atlantic steam shipping virtually begins with the Cunard Line's founding as far back as 1840 and continues today, albeit with combined diesel and gas turbine generated electrical propulsion rather than steam. Cunard's mail and passenger service was pre-dated by other ships, including the pioneering American steamship *Savannah* and Brunel's *Great Britain* that made successful crossings of the Western Ocean, though these were for the most part undertaken on an experimental basis. Samuel Cunard took the bold step of securing a mail contract from the Admiralty, and living up to his contractual obligations to the Crown on a solid commercial basis with his initial class building of four virtually identical wooden steam-powered paddle steamers.

From these humble, though nonetheless somewhat progressive beginnings, Cunard and the competitors that emerged at its side progressed to inevitably larger paddle wheelers, to screw propulsion, iron and then steel hulls, eventually doing away altogether with the auxiliary sailing rigs still carried and occasionally used aboard their earlier ships. The on board milieu advanced from the shipwright's art of the sailing packet era to the grandeur of the urban Grand Hotel with all of its creature comforts and *haut couture* architectural and decorative curlicues. Cunard lived its veritable adolescence through the marvellously progressive Victorian era before coming of age in the early 20th century with the remarkable steam-turbine, express liners *Mauretania* and *Lusitania*, followed in the year of World War I's outbreak by the magnificent *Aquitania* which served until 1950. The 20th century's remaining decades belonged to the 'Queens', first the pre-World War II launched *Queen Mary* and *Queen Elizabeth* and then from 1969 onwards the singularly iconic *Queen Elizabeth 2*. By the end of 1974 Cunard in effect had the remaining transatlantic trade to itself after ships such as the *United States*, *France* and *Rotterdam* were either laid up or switched to full-time cruising.

The *Queen Mary 2*'s planning and realisation is also the remarkable story of her principal designer, Stephen Payne, who embarked on his own life's career aspirations after visiting the *Queen Elizabeth 2* in Southampton at the age of nine, when he decided that he wanted to design and build great passenger ships such as this. Growing up and being educated at a time when passenger shipping seemed to be in decline, he faced considerable opposition to his aspirations. Through his own initiative and with the help of one of his teachers in particular, he ultimately succeeded and was chosen to head the project for building the ship that would ultimately replace the *Queen Elizabeth 2* and carry on her role into the 21st century. As the first true express ocean liner to be built in more than three decades, the *Queen Mary 2*'s planning and building called for a great deal of creative thinking, a sound knowledge of North Atlantic shipping as it was at the time of the *Queen Elizabeth 2* genesis, and the ingenuity to again combine the roles of line service and cruising, this time in the context of 21st century living. The *Queen Mary 2* is also the product of a globalised shipping industry where, though registered and home-ported in Britain, she is owned by the international and primarily American-based Carnival Corporation, designed in part by Swedish architects, powered by machinery of both British and Finnish origin and built in France at the same yard as the French Line's *Normandie* that was the old *Queen Mary*'s prime pre-War rival.

The *Queen Elizabeth 2* was sold and ended her service career in 2008 to take up a static role in Dubai for her new owners, leaving the new *Queen Mary 2* to continue the North Atlantic service that Sir Samuel Cunard had first inaugurated in 1840, bearing as did his first ships, the designation RMS (Royal Mail Ship). The Atlantic run is now seasonal, with the rest of the year spent cruising, and the RMS designation more honorary than being entirely functional as it was in earlier days. Yet, apart from wartimes, the North Atlantic route has been continuously served by Cunard Line ships now for more than 170 years. Also cut in the uniqueness of character as the *Queen Elizabeth 2*, the now eight-year-old *Queen Mary 2* is likewise already establishing herself worldwide as a veritable legend in her own time. She too possesses the 'aura of the singular' that was her predecessor's hallmark and that holds the fascination to bring people out from their beds before daybreak to greet her at ports and anchorages large and small wherever she calls on her worldwide voyages.

As we commence our literary and visual voyage aboard the *Queen Mary 2* through these 96 pages, we find ourselves in the milieu of the modern cruise industry, with the high proportions of luxury upper decks, veranda cabins, the spectacular atria, full-fledged theatres, alternative and specialty restaurants, health and spa facilities and other features demanded by today's passengers. Yet uniquely, aboard the *Queen Mary 2* these are packaged within a magnificently sturdy and seaworthy hull and superstructure formed and fabricated under the skilled hands of Stephen Payne and his colleagues at Carnival Corporation's Southampton offices and in the Chantiers de l'Atlantique shipyard (now part of STX Europe) in Saint-Nazaire, France.

The *Queen Mary 2*, for all of her modernity and technical advancement, is still at heart very much a Cunarder given the sense of tradition and history that she brings forward from her forebears, the old pre-War 'Queens' and the *Queen Elizabeth 2*. Perhaps most significantly, she represents an enduring element of Cunard's own company culture that has survived through the Line's tenure under Trafalgar House, the Kvaerner Group and ultimately its absorption into Carnival Corporation, and along with these changes, the relocation of its headquarters from Liverpool, first to Southampton, then to the United States. This is an enduring quality of being that has surely survived through the ships themselves, the long-serving officers and crew that have sailed them and cared for those who continue to sail with them, and in those passengers themselves who continue generation-by-generation to demand the uniquely Cunard way of life at sea with its oft-quaint British social institutions, its own resilient resourcefulness and its ever high level of personal service and attention.

Philip Dawson

The **Queen Mary 2** bids adieu to her birthplace in the Loire Estuary against a backdrop of the Pont de Saint-Nazaire and carrying a large banner that says "Merci Saint-Nazaire," as depicted in this Robert Lloyd painting.

CHAPTER 1

SOUTHAMPTON 1969

CUNARD

QUEEN MARY 2

During June 1969 a group of local tourists from Bournemouth on a coach tour of the Southampton region were treated to a tour of Cunard's then brand new *Queen Elizabeth 2* that happened to be in port alongside the Ocean Terminal that day as part of a regular turnaround between voyages during her second month in service. Even back then, before the airliner hijackings of the early 1970s, security was tight around the prestigious new transatlantic liner, and access to the ship other than for passengers and crew was something of a rarity, so these people were very fortunate that somehow arrangements were made for their visit to the ship. Among these were the Payne family, who at the time were holidaying in Bournemouth, with their nine-year-old son, Stephen, for whom the experience was ultimately to shape his life and future career.

Young Stephen was absolutely fascinated with all that he saw of the ultra-modern and highly sophisticated new *QE2*. He took in every detail of her decks, interiors, facilities and those working parts of the ship that were shown to the group during the hour or so they were aboard. He had already started to develop a keen interest in passenger ships two years earlier from having seen a short film feature on the popular BBC Television young people's programme 'Blue Peter', where an inbound Channel crossing on board the old *Queen Elizabeth* from Cherbourg to Southampton at the end of a regular line voyage from New York was shown by presenter Valerie Singleton who lamented to her viewers that the ship was about to be retired from service.[1] Already the French Line's last *France*, commissioned in 1962, had been described in the shipbuilding press as being a veritable 'never-never land' that sadly would likely be a 'never-again land' ever to be built,[2] and in 1969 the *QE2* was already being called 'the last great superliner'.

By 1972 the old *Queen Mary* was already in the static role she retains to this day as a tourist attraction and hotel in the

*Top: Stephen Payne on holiday on board the **Queen Elizabeth 2** off Cape Town, South Africa. (Stephen Payne collection)*

*Above: Stephen Payne as Chief Naval Architect and Director of Project Management for **Queen Mary 2's**, poses with a builders' model of his ship. (Stephen Payne)*

*The first **Queen Mary** 'dressed all over' with passengers at her deck rails and with onlookers aboard an excursion vessel seen at left as she is manoeuvred by*

...thampton. (John Hendy)

city of Long Beach, California. Her sister the *Queen Elizabeth* had originally been intended for a similar role in southern Florida, and ended up instead being purchased by the C.Y. Tung Group for conversion in Hong Kong as an ocean-going educational institution named *Seawise University*. As an ambitious interior remodelling for this purpose was nearing completion, fires broke out simultaneously in several locations on board the ship on 9th January 1972 causing her to eventually capsize onto her starboard side in Hong Kong's Victoria harbour. The wreck remained as a massive burnt-out and half-submerged hulk until 1974 before being declared a hazard to shipping and was finally broken up where she lay. The *United States* was withdrawn from service and entered into a purgatory of eternal lay-up that continues to the time of this being written. The only two other passenger ships built with the capability for sustained transatlantic service in the years immediately following the *QE2*'s debut were German Atlantic Line's *Hamburg*, delivered by the yard Howaldtswerke-Deutsche Werft in Kiel in the same year as the *QE2* and the British-built *Vistafjord*, completed by Swan Hunter for Norwegian America Line in 1973. Other passenger-ship building at the time was mostly car ferries and smaller cruise ships for short-duration tropical voyages developed more or less as an offshoot of these.

The trade journal *Shipbuilding and Shipping Record*'s extensive coverage of the *Queen Elizabeth 2* meanwhile was themed on presenting her as "a ship with a past...and a future."[3] This went into considerable detail about her design being influenced by the amassed liner-age experience of Cunard itself and its principal competitors and contemporaries, then most notably including ships such as Holland America's 1959-built, elegant and remarkably functional *Rotterdam*, French Line's elite *France* and the progressively innovative *Oriana* and *Canberra* built for the combined Australian and Far Eastern operations of Orient

*Above: As seen in this post-War view, at least four tugs were needed to manoeuvre the first **Queen Mary** in the days before transverse thrusters and azimuthing propulsion pods made it possible for large ships to dock and undock without assistance. (John Hendy)*

Line and P&O. The other side of the story was that Cunard's new *QE2* was designed also with a clear view to an emerging new era of luxury worldwide cruising. Where contingencies were made for this as a significant secondary role for ships such as *Rotterdam*, *France*, *Oriana* and *Canberra*, the new Cunard flagship was in fact planned firstly for cruising, with transatlantic line service being the secondary role.

At about three-quarters the size of her quadruple-screw predecessors, the *Queen Mary* and *Queen Elizabeth*, the more agile twin-propeller *Queen Elizabeth 2* was packaged up in a sleek and slender hull that had the look of a giant ocean-going yacht styled by prominent British architect James Gardner, and containing crisply modern architectural interiors coordinated by architect Dennis Lennon. The new

ship was absolutely stunning – perhaps in the eyes of some, too much so for a Cunarder. Widely acclaimed in various architectural and design publications including the *Architectural Review*, and in the popular press, she represented the best of contemporary 1960s British technology, design and style. It was no doubt this cachet of forward-focused modernity born into the rich tradition of the classic luxury international sea travel that appealed most to the young and fertile mind of Stephen Payne that summer day in Southampton, and that was the stuff of which his dreams were made for his own future as a designer of such ships.

Stephen quickly put the letter-writing skills he was learning at school to practical use contacting major shipping lines such as Cunard, French Line, Holland America and P&O about his interest in designing ships and even going so far as to submit some of his own ideas to them. When the 'Blue Peter Annual' of 1972 ran a tribute to the *Queen Elizabeth* following her loss in Hong Kong as *Seawise University*, concluding that "we shall never see her like again," Stephen wrote to convey his own opinion that he hoped someday he would build new passenger ships such as this, offering some ideas of what he envisaged for the future of passenger shipping. While the 'Blue Peter' people commended him for his enthusiasm and awarded him his first 'Blue Peter' badge for his efforts, they also expressed their view at the time that nobody foresaw much hope of anything so ambitious ever being built. Stephen fared better, however, in his correspondence with P&O and the ideas he had offered to them on ship design. He was given an interview with them at their Leadenhall Street headquarters in London's City district. As Stephen was only 11 years old at the time, his mother accompanied him to London. They were both warmly received by the P&O people who were quite amazed to find that they had been dealing with so young a person, though they nonetheless showed interest in his future, encouraging him in the meantime to pursue an academic line of education and to keep in touch with them.

After leaving his London secondary comprehensive school in 1977, Stephen enrolled in a university degree course studying chemistry and physics, following a general academic path recommended by his teachers who had by then convinced him that there was little likelihood of him ever making a living designing ships. During his first year Stephen's career aspirations were rescued by his physics teacher, Justin Johnson, who realised he was unhappy with the choice he had ended up with, and helped him to secure an additional year's grant and switch to the Ship Science course at Southampton University.

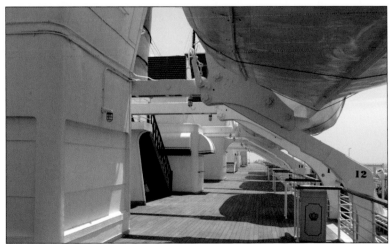

Top: The first **Queen Mary** *as she appears today at 75 years of age in her static role as a hotel and tourist attraction at Long Beach California, showing the Verandah Grill restaurant overlooking the ship's afterdecks. (Miles Cowsill)*

Above: The handsome and wide boat deck, still looking much as it did 75 years ago, though now with the 'California touch' of the crown-monogrammed

*Above: Still impressive in their romantic portrayal of the traditional liner image, the first **Queen Mary**'s funnels are now lightweight facsimiles replacing the originals that were removed shortly after the ship's 1967 arrival at Long Beach. (Miles Cowsill)*

For his study project at Southampton he chose to design a hypothetical passenger ship based on specifications given to him by P&O during his ongoing correspondence with them. His professors were concerned about his having chosen so complex and sophisticated a project and encouraged him to perhaps undertake something less ambitious. Yet Stephen remained adamant that it was passenger ships that interested him most, and that it was these that he wanted to design in his future career. After completing his project and graduating with high honours, Stephen felt that his degree was "mostly theoretical"[4] and that to design ships he still needed to learn from "getting on a boat or a ship and seeing what happens when you turn the rudder." For the opportunity he needed to get his hands on real ships and to get some practical seafaring experience he signed up with the University Royal Navy Unit where he served as a midshipman with the minesweeper *Woodlark*.

After completing his tour of duty with the Royal Navy, Stephen then worked ashore for Marconi Marine on contract bidding for naval replenishment ships, before being contacted in 1984 by Jacob Victor of the naval architectural firm Technical Marine Planning (TMP) with his first offer of work in the passenger ship field. This was in fact in reply to an application he had made some time earlier. TMP had been involved with Carnival Cruises since the beginning when they made the initial surveys of the former Canadian Pacific liner *Empress of Canada* acquired and later converted as the first 'Carnival Fun Ship' *Mardi Gras* in 1972. Carnival had since acquired the also laid up *Empress of Britain* and *SA Vaal*, introducing these into an emerging new Miami-based cruise market as *Carnivale* and *Festivale* respectively. In 1981 Carnival introduced its first purpose-built new cruise ship the Danish-built *Tropicale* from Aalborg Waerft. This was followed by the slightly larger *Holiday* from the same yard and the nearly identical *Jubilee* and *Celebration* from Cockums in Malmö, Sweden.

These, along with the *Atlantic* for Home Lines, Holland America's *Nieuw Amsterdam* and *Noordam* and Hapag-Lloyd's *Europa* were all in the 30,000 to 45,000 GT (gross ton) range and delivered in the early 1980s as the first of a progression to liner-size cruise ships and ultimately far beyond even the sizes of the *Normandie* and the old Cunard 'Queens'. Stephen's first activities at TMP included trim and stability calculations for the *Holiday* as well as on-site inspections of the ship's building. He was well on his way to achieving his dream, though at that stage nobody could have foreseen that Carnival would later own Costa, Cunard, Holland America, Princess and P&O Cruises, and that he really would end up designing ships for these lines far larger then the *QE2* that had inspired his dream and fired his imagination that day in Southampton during the summer of 1969.

Crossing to cruising

The years 1957 and 1958 were a significant turning point for the passenger shipping business, when the steamship lines and the airlines each carried just over a million passengers on their respective North Atlantic services in 1957. From then onwards the airline figures grew and the numbers of passengers travelling by sea went into a steady decline. The 1962 figures showed two million passengers crossing by air and only 800 thousand by sea.[5] While the number of people travelling by air had doubled in five years, those crossing by sea had diminished by only 20 per cent, showing in fact an overall exponential growth in overseas travel. The industry was becoming more diversified in providing alternatives both for those wanting swift passage from one place to another and others wishing to take advantage of the travel experience itself by opting to sail rather than fly. As the introduction in 1958 of the Boeing

Above: The first Queen Mary's foredecks, superstructure and bridge front, as these can now be viewed by visitors to the ship, from a vantage point out of bounds to passengers during the Queen Mary's service career. (Miles Cowsill)

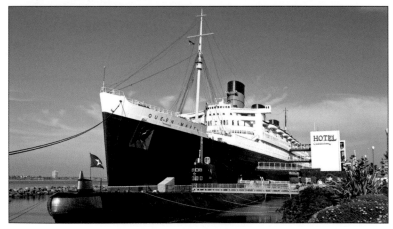

*Top: The first **Queen Mary**'s navigating bridge, with its total lack of computers and other digital equipment, remains static in a time warp of the years she served, though remarkably with her mechanical engine telegraphs set to indicate full speed ahead. (Miles Cowsill)*

*Above: As she appears today, the first **Queen Mary** remains eternally linked to the access tower, mid right, which is a Building Code requirement of her role as a static land-based attraction. (Miles Cowsill)*

707 jet airliner reduced the flying time between London or Paris and New York to a mere eight hours without the need for refuelling and service stops at Shannon, Gander or Goose Bay, flying suddenly became far more comfortable and attractive to the travelling public. While this was an especially great advantage to business travellers, it also made overseas holiday travel possible for North American wage earners who typically only received two-to-three weeks of paid vacation time per year, though jet air travel remained costly and elitist until economy class was later introduced. The 'jet set' was also provided with spectacular new passenger terminal facilities, offering fine restaurants, tax-free shopping and other services, at London-Heathrow, Paris-Orly, New York-Idlewind (later JFK) and other key international airports.

Meanwhile, at sea level the comparatively new phenomenon of the drive-aboard car-passenger ferry, or roll-on roll-off (ro-ro) ferry as it is widely known, was beginning to radically change the public's perception of shipboard comfort and service. The Denny-built *Maid of Kent*, with her attractively functional modern interiors designed by the noted British design firm of Ward & Austin, was among the first to give the post-World War II travelling public a taste of a more contemporary and informal shipboard experience when introduced on British Rail's Sealink Dover to Boulogne route in 1959. Larger Sealink ships built during the 1960s, including the *Avalon* built for overnight Continental service between Harwich to Hoek van Holland and the domestic Stranraer-Larne *Caledonian Princess*, asserted an even greater sense of sophistication, comfort and luxury on a par with the best new deep-sea liners then also going into intercontinental services around the globe.

Other modern ferries of the time were built for far longer routes, such as the service jointly operated by the Italian Adriatica di Navigazione's purpose-built ferry *Appia* and her Greek-flag Hellenic Mediterranean Line's counterpart

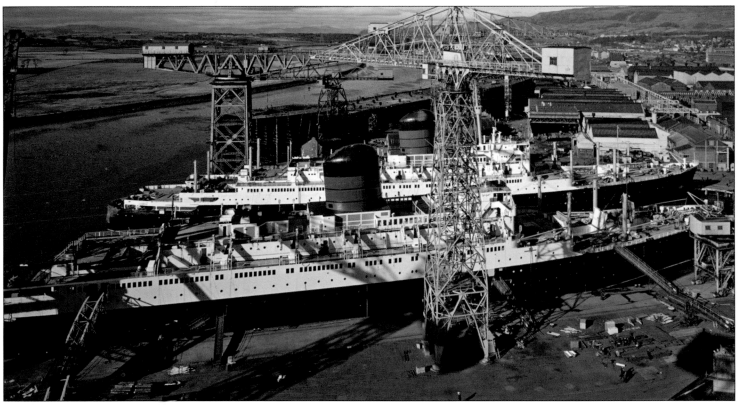

*Above: Cunard's intermediate North Atlantic liners **Saxonia** and **Ivernia** returned to their birthplace on the Clyde in 1963 to be converted for cruising as the **Carmania** and **Franconia** respectively. (Bruce Peter collection)*

Egnatia, sailing from the Italian Adriatic port of Brindisi to Corfu, Igoumenitsa and Patras. The year-round service was heavily patronised by tourists, from those travelling with their own vehicles and taking cabin accommodation on board to backpackers and other foot passengers, all of whom could enjoy the crossing as something of a short international cruise experience. The Israeli Somerfin Line's *Bilu* and *Nili* were purpose built in 1964-5 for a similar style of service on the longer two-and-a-half-day route between Naples and Haifa via Piraeus and Limassol. Only the *Nili* actually went into this service, which was operated through the summer of

1964, before she was transferred to Miami for a winter season of alternating three- and four-night voyages to the Bahamian ports of Freeport and Nassau and to Montego Bay in Jamaica, returning to the Mediterranean the following summer on the longer route between Nice and Haifa. Originally intended to open a new service between Southampton and Algeciras, the *Nili* was, however, immediately chartered in 1965 to Finnlines for the prestigious Hansa Route peak-season service between Helsinki and the West German port of Travemünde as a stand-in for the line's own new ferry *Finnhansa* which had

*Top: Known as the Green Goddess for her distinctive green hull and superstructure paint scheme, Cunard's **Caronia** was delivered in 1949 as a fleet mate to the second **Mauretania** for high-season Atlantic service and luxury cruising the rest of the year. (John Hendy collection)*

*Above: The Swedish Lloyd ferry **Saga**, seen here, and **Patricia** were car ferries built for cruise-style service on the longer Gothenburg-Tilbury and Southampton-Santander routes. (Bruce Peter collection)*

been seriously damaged by fire during her fitting out.

Longer car-passenger ferry services from the British Isles included a two-night crossing between Gothenburg and the British ports of Hull and London-Tilbury operated jointly by Swedish Lloyd's *Saga* in tandem with the *Spero* of British-owned Ellerman Wilson Line. By 1967 new routes were also opened between Southampton and Santander with Swedish Lloyd's *Patricia*, joined later by P&O's *Eagle*. These, along with various overnight crossings such as TT Line's Harwich to Hamburg and Bremerhaven and other routes could also be booked as so-called 'mini-cruise' round-trip excursions, giving many ordinary citizens the opportunity to sample a remarkably affordable liner-like cruise experience over a weekend.

What these people discovered aboard the new car-passenger ferries was a level of comfort and service comparable to many deep-sea ocean liners of that time, though with service and passenger care presented on a considerably more modern and informal basis. Dining arrangements were more along the lines of contemporary hospitality ashore, with flexible mealtimes, open seating arrangements and usually a choice of à la carte, al fresco or smorgasbord service. Modern open-plan public spaces were elegant, bright and for the most part informal. In most instances passengers were carried in a single class, giving them the full run of the ship and its facilities. On the longer Adriatic, Baltic and Eastern Mediterranean routes there was a greater emphasis on railway-style couchettes and liner-style cabin accommodation for the majority of passengers, with reclining airline seats continuing to be offered for those wanting to travel without cabins, effectively as deck passengers, at lower cost.

The Somerfin services to Haifa and the Finnish Hansa Route ferries were among the most sophisticated of these in their time. The trade journal *The Motor Ship* described the

Nili as: "a miniature passenger liner [that] could be used for cruising anywhere in the world."[6] Most outstanding among these was the *Finlandia*, as a larger and more luxurious version of the *Finhansa* and *Finnpartner* delivered in 1967 to the Finland Steamship Company for their own rival two-night service between Travemünde and Helsinki, by way of Copenhagen. Indeed a number of these ships, including Somerfin's *Nili* and the *Sunward*, originally intended for a Kloster Rederi service from Southampton to Vigo, Lisbon and Gibraltar, ended up in Miami-based Caribbean cruise service. The *Sunward* in particular set the standards of design and service for Kloster-owned Norwegian Caribbean Line's (NCL's) first-generation *White Fleet* that came on-stream in the early 1970s. Ships such as these brought the essence of an exclusive Scandinavian Swedish-American Line or Norwegian America Line style and service to within reach of the average family wanting to take a short and inexpensive cruise holiday.

As the established deep-sea steamship companies continued to build prestigious new liners during the 1960s, many of these were designed with a view to alternative cruising roles in the off-peak season and ultimately even for permanent use if the original line trades were to dry up during their service-life expectancies of 25 to 35 years. At the time this gesture of diversity was foreseen as being mainly a matter of adding swimming pools and lidos on deck and being able to easily combine the divergent first and tourist-class public rooms needed in class-segregated line service so as to give all passengers a full run of the ship while cruising. Aboard Holland America's *Rotterdam* of 1959 and the French Line's *France* completed three years later this was done by arranging the lounges, bars and other facilities for each class on separate decks, one above the other, and either combining or separating these one from the other by way of access to the separate stairways and passenger lifts designated for the

Top: British Rail Sealink's **Avalon** *was a pioneer in introducing a modern liner style of service when she made her debut on the overnight Harwich-Hook of Holland ferry service in 1959. (Ferry Publications collection)*

Above: Built for the Esbjerg-Harwich route, the DFDS ferry **Winston Churchill** *featured a high standard of on-board design by Danish architect Kay Kørbing. (Bruce Peter collection)*

*Top: The Soviet five-ship **Ivan Franko** class was built in the mid 1960s to provide affordable passage on various routes around the world including North Atlantic service from northern Europe to Montreal and New York. (FotoFlite)*

*Above: P&O's **Canberra**, arriving in the Solent on her return from the Falklands War in 1982. (FotoFlite)*

two classes. P&O and Orient's *Oriana* and aft-engined *Canberra* of the same era were each arranged with all first-class facilities forward and tourist class aft, so that combining the two was a matter of merely opening connecting doors amidships between the two zones. Public rooms aboard the *Eugenio C* were likewise arranged with first class forward and tourist aft on the promenade deck, though with first-class cabins and suites above along the length of the boat and sun decks above them with tourist accommodations amidships and aft along three hull decks beneath the dining rooms.

The fore-and-aft approach was also adopted in the rather loosely defined class barriers of Swedish-American Line's last *Gripsholm* and *Kungsholm*, implemented more to meet North Atlantic Passenger Conference regulations than to serve any real practical purpose in service. Shaw Savill's aft-engined *Southern Cross* and *Northern Star* and the Union Castle Line's *Transvaal Castle* were designed for line service with all passengers accommodated in a single class. Initially intended for North Atlantic service as a predominantly tourist-class ship with exclusive accommodation including eight veranda cabins for a small number of first-class passengers, the Home Lines' *Oceanic* was delivered in 1965 for one-class service in full-time cruising.

While a nominal gesture towards cruising was made through the addition of pools, other outdoor recreational facilities and the amalgamation of public spaces; the standard and character of cabin accommodation remained rooted in the idea of line service, with large numbers of small inside cabins without portholes or windows and with fixed upper and lower berths. The standards were highest on transatlantic ships such as the *Rotterdam* and *France* where virtually all cabins in both classes had their own en-suite toilets, with the rooms themselves being generally more spacious and close carpeted throughout. (The *Rotterdam* originally had a small number of minimum-rate rooms without their own toilet facilities that were later upgraded.) Although also offering a similarly high standard of first-class accommodation, the *Oriana* and *Canberra* were in reality built primarily for the Australian emigrant trade, having large numbers of tiny four-berth tourist class rooms without private toilet facilities. With a view to off-season cruising, a number of these were ingeniously fitted out to convert quickly from a four-berth accommodation without facilities to a room for two in upper and lower berths and a compact toilet unit. Following the example of American railway sleeping car design, a steward could make the changeover by folding away one set of upper and lower berths revealing the plumbing fixtures and pulling out a sliding partition with a door in it to separate the shower and toilet from the room with the remaining two berths.

While the Americans enthusiastically welcomed the *Oriana* and *Canberra* with their crisply modern open-plan public interiors, vast amounts of open deck space, outdoor recreation facilities and myriad technical innovativeness, during their maiden calls to the West Coast ports of San Francisco and Los Angeles in 1960 and 1961 and during a visit the *Canberra* made to New York in 1962, they were generally less enthusiastic about actually booking space in the lower-grade tourist accommodations of either ship. Both P&O Orient Line ships later became hugely popular in the British home-market cruise trade, with the *Canberra* serving until the end of the 1997 summer high season.

Against the march of progress in modern liner and car-passenger ferry design, Cunard's venerable and much-loved *Queen Mary* and *Queen Elizabeth* appeared decidedly dated, stuffy and overly formal by comparison. Both ships were refitted and modernised in an effort to bring them up to post-War service standards. Anti-rolling stabilisers, swimming pools and lido decks were added to the five-years-younger *Queen Elizabeth* with a view to a secondary cruising role for

Top: With machinery aft and tall 'goal-post' funnels, Holland America's **Rotterdam** *symbolised the re-emergence of the Netherlands and Western Europe in the progressively modern post-World War 2 era. (Author's collection)*

Above: Completed in 1952, the **United States** *was a one-off leviathan without a compatible fleet mate until operationally becoming a half-sister to French Line's* **France***, with which she sailed transatlantic on alternating weeks until being laid up in 1969. (FotoFlite)*

her. Yet both ships seemed destined to remain locked into the time warp of 1930s social institutions and grand-luxe travel in which they were originally built. They were simply too large and too grand for the jet age.

Cunard had already started to think about the next generation of ships that would ultimately replace these when preliminary sketches and drawings were first prepared by the line's technical department as early as 1951. Perhaps it was no coincidence that this happened during the year of the Festival of Britain, which marked the 1851 Great Exhibition's centenary and aimed at stimulating a sense of redevelopment and progress throughout Britain in the aftermath of World War II. It also aimed at promoting modern British design in all things from the architecture of new towns and buildings to industrial and consumer products, fashion and the graphic arts. While the architecturally most progressive new British liners at the time were the New Zealand Shipping Company's 1949-built *Rangitoto* and *Rangitane*, the *United States*, then being fitted out at Newport News, Virginia, provided the most modern and advanced example of the type of ship needed for post-War express North Atlantic service. The American ship was being built to an underlying US Navy structural and engineering standard for alternate use as a fast troop transport if needed as such in times of war, inevitably with some compromise to the higher standards of traditional passenger comfort and luxury to which Cunard still aspired. By 1958 these original concepts for ships to replace the 'Queens' had gelled into the basis of detailed plans for what was essentially to have been a larger Cunard rendition of the *United States* code-named 'Q3' (the third 'Queen'). This all took place during a time when the demand for sea travel was still high, sustaining a year-round North Atlantic trade still fairly solidly committed to a traditional three-class style of accommodation and service.

The 'Q3' project was scrapped on the eve of a contract being signed with John Brown for the ship's building, and was ultimately succeeded by the more contemporary conception for a fourth ship, first code-named 'Q4' and launched in September 1967 as *Queen Elizabeth 2*. Scaled down to the approximate size range of the *United States*, this was to be a more agile twin-screw dual-purpose ship equally capable of peak summer-season line service on the North Atlantic run and of worldwide luxury cruising for the rest of the year. The 'Q4' was designed with a dominant aluminium superstructure, similar to those of P&O's then recently built *Oriana* and *Canberra*, providing the weight economy to include one more deck than would have been possible with steel construction, and with an ultra-compact steam turbine propulsion plant yielding a 28.5-knot service speed for Atlantic crossings and other long sea passages as well as economical operation at the lower speeds used in cruise service. Cunard had originally insisted that a three-class service was expected by their passengers in North Atlantic line service, as then still provided by United States Lines and Italia, despite the trend towards a more flexible two-class arrangement of newer Atlantic liners such as the *Rotterdam* and *France*.

While Cunard had already adopted a fairly modern design approach as far back as the more advanced planning stage of the 'Q3', concern was expressed from within West End London's design and high-society circles that the line's new flagship should be nothing less than a bold expression of the era's modernity with a deftly British spin. These people felt that other recently built British ships such as Union Castle Line's *Transvaal Castle* and *Windsor Castle*, though modern, were still too eclectic, while the open planning and crisply clean-lined modernity of P&O Orient Line's *Oriana* and *Canberra* were too informal for the perceived role as a sea-going ambassador of British design and industrial progress foreseen for the new Cunard ship. Since the government was backing the project with loan guarantees, the matter was even raised in parliamentary debate at Westminster, with the result that eventually the Council of Industrial Design was asked to advise Cunard on their ultimate choice of designers for the *QE2*. James Gardner, one of the principal coordinating architects for the Festival of Britain, was retained in his role in styling the ship's exterior, with Dennis Lennon given charge over the interior architecture handled by a cadre of prominent designers whose work was characteristically progressive without being too avant-garde or trendy.

Thanks to a six-month delay in the *QE2*'s completion as a result of industrial actions and shortages of skilled labour, Cunard had the opportunity to significantly rethink the design and arrangement of the ship's public rooms more along the lines of those aboard the two-class *Rotterdam* and *France*. They also went the additional step of following Swedish-American Line's 1958 *Gripsholm* example to arrange these firstly for open-class cruising, with a loosely defined two-class designation of the Quarter and Upper deck rooms for North Atlantic service. The revised *QE2* plan featured a broad range of different public spaces, each with its own purpose and atmosphere, and the flexibility to also offer spaces of similar function though differing in character for first- and tourist-class passengers during Atlantic crossings.

For example, the Queens Room, designed primarily as a traditional ballroom, served alternatively as the first-class main lounge. The vast Double Room was conceived by its designer, Jon Bannenberg, as "a room in which many people could be doing many things...and yet one not have to disturb the other,"[7] and also became the main tourist-class lounge on the North Atlantic run. Likewise, the Q4 Room had a double life as the tourist-class nightclub and as the lido bar in cruise service while the 736 Club did evening duty as a discotheque while serving as a daytime café.[8] The *QE2* was also among

*Top: Completed in 1951 for passenger and cargo service around Africa, Union Castle Line's **Rhodesia Castle** set a good example of early post-War tropical passenger service, though without being designed for cruising per se. (FotoFlite)*

*Above: The Pacific Steam Navigation Company ship **Reina del Mar** of 1956 as she appeared after her 1964 conversion for cruising, where she gained great popularity in the British market until she was scrapped in 1975. (FotoFlite)*

23

*Top: The **France's** extensive conversion for full-time cruising as the **Norway** was of key significance in showing that large-ship cruising was to be the way of the future. (Miles Cowsill)*

*Above: The former Swedish-American Line **Kungsholm's** conversion for cruising as the **Sea Princess** was a commercial success. (FotoFlite)*

the first passenger ships where provision was made for professional entertainment, with a number of spaces such as the Queen's and Double Rooms having slightly raised floor levels in their periphery areas to improve sightlines to the stage, and with production lighting and sound systems being installed as part of the ship's outfitting. Although fairly traditional by today's standards, the cabins were also designed with an emphasis on cruising, with three-quarters of these having portholes or windows in the ship's sides and side-by-side beds being preferred over upper and lower berths.

Cruising comes of age

At the time of her long-awaited April 1969 debut in commercial service Cunard's *Queen Elizabeth 2* was without doubt the most advanced and sophisticated passenger ship ever to have been built. When nine-year-old Stephen Payne visited the ship two months later in Southampton with his parents and younger siblings, the impressions he took home that day definitely offered a massive perspective into a bright future for the passenger shipping industry that few then had the vision to grasp and comprehend. Most people were then lamenting the withdrawals from service of favoured ships and the winding down of the stalwart and well-known steamship companies that had once owned and operated them. Popular perception was that the airlines were killing off sea travel. Yet lines such as Swedish-American, Holland America, Costa and P&O Orient were redeploying their fleets ever more to full-time cruising and would soon enough be looking to the airlines as providers of airlift power to bring cruise passengers across the continent to their ships.

The *QE2*'s influence on cruising was almost immediate, with the *Royal Viking Star*, *Royal Viking Sky* and *Royal Viking Sea*, likewise built for worldwide luxury cruising showing a

*Above: Seen here as the **SA Vaal** against a backdrop of Table Mountain in Cape Town, Union Castle's **Transvaal Castle** of 1961 was progressively planned with all passengers carried in a single 'hotel class'. (FotoFlite)*

marked resemblance to the *QE2* funnel and a similarity in the key elements of their overall interior layout with their main dining rooms located on the upper decks as early as 1971-3 when these were delivered. The lounge deck layouts of these followed the *QE2*'s Quarter Deck plan, with the galley fully forward, followed by the dining room and main lounge amidships and a pool lido aft most. The cabins aboard these were generally larger than those of similar ships derived from the modern ferry model then being built for seven-night tropical cruises in the service of other lines such as Royal Caribbean and Norwegian Caribbean.

The *Cunard Adventurer* and *Cunard Ambassador* were

completed at the same time as smaller fleet mates to the *QE2*, giving Cunard its own presence in the emerging mass-market tropical cruise trade. Although these were originally ordered and construction started for another owner from the United States, their exteriors were nonetheless styled by James Gardner, following on from his success with the *QE2*. When the original owner's venture fell through, the two hulls were purchased by Cunard and completed to Gardner's original design.[9] The singularly distinctive appearance of these, with tall funnels having the unusual backward rake of the *QE2*'s mast, and with the bridge and superstructure front, clearly showed the influence of Gardner's earlier work for Cunard

Above: The **Queen Elizabeth 2** *as she appeared in 1982 after the Falkland Islands conflict, with her hull painted pebble grey and her original slender black-and-white funnel in traditional Cunard red and black. (FotoFlite)*

yet without going so far as to be viewed as being replicated or copied from it.

When Stephen Payne received his first pay cheque as a practising naval architect in 1984, the modern cruise industry was already progressing to its second generation of new ships. Among the initial wave of these was Carnival's first purpose-built *Tropicale*, a pivotal ship that would establish a particular style and way of doing things for the line, and ultimately set standards for the whole industry. With its earlier conversion of the *SA Vaal* as the *Festivale*, Carnival had acquired a ship with a vast amount of cargo space on its lower decks that was unsuitable for being turned into passenger accommodation, but useful as handling areas for baggage and ship's stores. Similar working spaces were included in the *Tropicale* with side access at pier height so that stores and baggage could be easily worked using portable conveyors and forklift trucks during short port turnarounds and then distributed aboard the ship after sailing. The *Tropicale* was also first to introduce a cabaret-style show lounge with an inclined floor and raked seating, and hence the 'crooked' row of cascading windows in the ship's sides that, along with the big gull-winged funnel became hallmark features of the Carnival Fun Ships.

By that time the *France* had been bought by Knut Kloster after five years of lay-up at Le Havre following her 1974 withdrawal from French Line service and extensively converted at Lloyd Werft in Bremerhaven for cruising under the Norwegian Caribbean Line house flag as the *Norway*. Along with the addition of spacious lidos and sun decks aft and atop the superstructure, the ship's interiors were significantly restyled for year-round cruising. The original first- and tourist-class public suites were integrated into a cohesive suite of spaces, with the first-class lounge on Verandah Deck converted into a nightclub, while the tourist, or *Rive Gauch* (Left Bank) as French Line called it, smoking room directly below on Promenade Deck became the casino. Since enclosed promenade decks were hardly needed in cruise service, those on Verandah Deck were turned into fully climate-controlled *QE2*-style periphery circulating arteries among the public spaces at that level. The tourist promenades below were taken over for luxury suites with panoramic windows similar to those that had already been added aboard the German liner *Hamburg* before she was sold to the Soviets and renamed *Maxim Gorkiy* for cruising in the German market under the hammer and cycle.

By the mid 1980s Royal Caribbean went into head-to-head competition with Norwegian Caribbean's *Norway* on the basis of size and capacity with their *Sovereign of the Seas*, completed in 1987. She was followed by a number of other ships in the same and similar classes for Royal Caribbean, as well as Carnival Cruises' own venture into larger tonnage with the 70,000-ton *Fantasy* completed in 1990. This was the first building project where Stephen Payne was involved from its outset, starting with the model basin and wind tunnel testing during the ship's formative design stages. Here Stephen also went on to develop his own ideas for the distinctive large bay window arrangement of the mid-body lido cantilever that also extended down to the public areas on the deck below. Altogether eight ships were built in the *Fantasy* class for Carnival between 1990 and 1998. The final two of these, the *Elation* and *Paradise*, were the first Carnival cruise ships where conventional rudders and shaft-driven propellers were done away with in favour of modern external azimuthing propulsion pods of the type later used for Cunard's *Queen Mary 2* in lieu of conventional shaft-driven propellers.

Meanwhile two more decks were added atop the *Norway*'s superstructure, maintaining her standing as 'the world's biggest' against the impending deliveries of other large new ships through the 1990s, until the first 100,000-tonners made their debut in 1996-7. At a volumetric measure of just over

Above: The **Queen Elizabeth 2** *after her 1986-87 conversion to diesel electric propulsion sporting an altogether larger funnel and with Quarter and Upper Decks extended farther aft to enclose added public spaces and more veranda cabins added topsides. (FotoFlite)*

100,000 tons each, *Carnival Destiny* and *Grand Princess* were the first passenger ships ever to eclipse the 80,000-ton *Normandie*, *Queen Mary* and *Queen Elizabeth* built more than 50 years earlier.

Miami-based Carnival Corporation, parent of Carnival Cruise Lines, had made an Initial Public Offering amounting to 20 per cent of the company's common stock on the American Exchange in 1987 to raise capital for expansion and to acquire Holland America Line, along with its subsidiaries Windstar Cruises and Holland America Tours in 1989 as well as Seabourn Cruises. Holland America's *Statendam* and *Carnival Destiny* were designed as a collaboration of the new Carnival Corporate shipbuilding group and Fincantieri Monfalcone Yard where these ships were built. The *Statendam* was in fact Fincantieri's first of many ships built at both their Monfalcone and Marghera yards for the Carnival Group. Carnival later set up its own Technical Services group based in London, bringing in-house the work previously done by Technical Marine Planning and acquiring Stephen Payne to become the group's chief naval architect.

At the age of 30 Stephen Payne was already living his life's dream. In addition to his work for Carnival, he also maintained an avid fascination with passenger ships and shipping, travelling often on ships unrelated to his work that especially interested him. Even before Holland America became part of the Carnival fold, the 1959-delivered *Rotterdam* had become a favourite of his. Stephen was very grateful to Carnival's founder, the late Ted Arison for giving him the opportunity and indeed the privilege of bringing the new Holland America *Rotterdam* into reality in 1997. He also became proactively involved in the effort to preserve the Royal Yacht *Britannia* due to be withdrawn from service in 1997. He had first become interested in the Royal Yacht while serving as a Royal Navy midshipman aboard the *Woodlark* through his Commanding Officer who had previously served aboard the *Britannia*. Stephen also found time to write and lecture, producing a book on the Holland America *Rotterdam* of 1959 as well as a number of academic and technical papers on ship design for the Royal Institution of Naval Architects, and commercial articles for the shipbuilding press including some material done jointly by Swedish ShipPax Information's publications with this author. Apart from speaking regularly at various professional and trade conferences, he also enjoys doing entertainment speaking for passengers while travelling at sea, and is interested to meet with other passengers who share his fascination with ships and the sea.

Apart from the inevitable march of progress towards ever-larger ships, one of the most significant cruise-ship developments was, however, the smaller 45,000-ton *Royal Princess*, designed to provide virtually all passengers with outer cabins having either large picture windows or private verandas. This was accomplished by a complete overturning of conventional passenger-ship design, with the hull decks housing the accommodations and the public rooms located above on the superstructure decks. The *QE2*, with the rationale of her clean break between three public decks atop five strata of suites and cabins on the hull decks was described in 1969 by Sir Hugh Casson as "an hotel on its head: four decks of public rooms of great variety of size and character, above five decks of bedrooms."[10] Fifteen years later the *Royal Princess* in effect turned the hotel right-side up again, with the public rooms inside her hull and five strata of hotel bedrooms, about half of them with their own private verandas in her superstructure. When the *Royal Princess* was delivered to Princess Cruises for American West Coast-based service in late 1984, her hotel-block approach soon set a new design standard for cruise ships. The *Carnival Destiny* and *Grand Princess* classes were among the first to adopt this approach on a large scale, significantly increasing the proportion of rooms with their own private verandas to as much as 90 per cent, as these became the most sought-after feature in modern cruising.

Succession of a Cunard 'Queen'

By the mid 1980s the *Queen Elizabeth 2* was nearing the middle of her anticipated service life, having already become one of the best-known and most-loved liners of all time, despite several highly embarrassing total losses of power and other mechanical problems while at sea. She had nonetheless achieved what might be best described as 'the aura of the singular', based on the German cultural theorist Walter Benjamin's notion of 'aura' in the context of an original masterwork of art, as an industrial or technological achievement that is in itself uplifting to behold and experience, and where the copying or replication of the original brainchild only ever produces at best an approximate or pale facsimile of it. The *QE2*'s exterior appearance, as styled by James Gardner, gave the comparatively large ship the distinctive stance of a graceful mega yacht that was unique for a ship of her size. It was absolutely iconic in its own right, like for example, the E-type Jaguar automobile. P&O's *Canberra* perhaps came closest to the *QE2* iconic singularity in the modern marine world for her own remarkable qualities of line and form, though as a ship that seldom crossed the North Atlantic or ventured into American cruising waters, she was less well known the world over.

Throughout her life the *QE2* was constantly being refitted and modified, both inside and out, to meet the perceived needs and expectations of the emerging luxury cruise market. Deluxe veranda suites were added atop her superstructure, the restaurants were re-configured,

Top: The **Queen Elizabeth 2** *fostered an altogether more modern on-board environment, with less extravagant use of space that was designed on a more human scale as seen on D stairway Quarter Deck. (Miles Cowsill)*

Above: Space age avant-garde in 1969, the **Queen Elizabeth 2***'s elegant Queen's Room attained a sense of classic timelessness as the ship aged and mellowed through her career of nearly 40 years. (Miles Cowsill)*

*Above: Compared with the boat deck views from the original **Queen Mary** on page 13, the **Queen Elizabeth 2**'s boat deck reflects a more efficient use of space aboard the newer ship. (Miles Cowsill)*

entertainment facilities restyled and alas, the élan of her original West End London *Sixties Mod* interiors were gradually subdued into a more generic international hotelier scenography that neither enthrals nor offends anybody.

Externally, the ship took on added mass, becoming also a bit lumpy here and there with the addition of veranda suites, modifications to the original superstructure front, extensions to the afterdecks and a much portlier funnel in traditional Cunard red and black. Yet throughout her long career of nearly 40 years, the *QE2* retained the remarkable 'aura' to draw people out of their beds in the predawn darkness of wherever she called to watch her arrival and to stay out late in the evening to see her off again. While other ships such as French Line's pre-War *Normandie*, or even the more contemporary example of her successor, *France*, Holland America's 1959 *Rotterdam* and Costa's *Eugenio C*, which featured remarkable axial interior layouts and spectacular modern *couture* Italian design, these retained a more conventional external appearance, even if they had modern goal-post funnels three-quarters aft, whereas the *QE2*'s profile was always absolutely unmistakable, even when viewed through haze on a distant horizon at sea.

The *QE2* was completely re-engined over the winter of 1986-7, converting her from steam to diesel-electric power, and along with other work done at the same time assuring her of another 20 years' service, Cunard would eventually have to start thinking of a replacement ship as they had done for the old 'Queens' in the 1950s. Through refits and refurbishment the ship was continuing to hold her just place at the forefront of luxury worldwide cruising, with the addition of such things as alternative dining, extended fitness and spa facilities and even a rather luxurious token gesture towards private-veranda staterooms, with these added atop her decks in several stages. Despite successive restyling and reconfiguring of her interiors and accommodations, there were some shortcomings beyond the scope of mere remedial renovation work.

Although the *QE2* was built with a large double-height auditorium similar to those aboard the 1959-built *Rotterdam* and the *France* of three years later, this was never adapted for cabaret shows as was done when the *France* was converted for full-time cruising as the *Norway*. Entertainment features of this sort aboard the *QE2* were usually presented in the Double Room, later modified for this purpose as the Grand Lounge. The ship was also unable to offer a complete single-sitting evening dining service like many of her newer upmarket competitors, and perhaps most seriously of all, she lacked by far sufficient numbers of veranda cabins to satisfy the, at least perceived, demand for them. Inevitably it is lifestyle and service issues such as these, rather than the failure of the structural elements such as the hull and superstructure, or of propelling machinery and other technical infrastructures that eventually court planning for the replacement even of such outstanding ships as the *QE2*.

Cunard had started thinking about their options beyond the *QE2*'s foreseeable lifespan since the early 1980s. Their decision to re-engine the ship mid decade bought them additional time to consider their options over the longer term of up to 20 years. During the 1990s the line's technical department began to plan a highly ambition new dual-purpose express liner and cruise ship of around 90,000 tons code-named 'Q5', with a maximum service speed of 40 knots and accommodation for 2,500 passengers. The work was done under great secrecy in partnership with the prominent Finnish marine and engineering consultancy Deltamarin. The plan was that the new ship would take over the *QE2*'s seasonal transatlantic services, relegating her to a full-time cruising role. If built, this ship would have come close to the long-classified performance of the *United States* in her alternative role as a fast troop transport. Although planned

Top: The **Cunard Adventurer**, seen here, and her sister **Cunard Ambassador** were the ships that made Cunard's initial entry into the modern American-based cruise business, following immediately on the cachet of the **Queen Elizabeth 2's** debut in 1969. (Bruce Peter collection)

Above: The former Norwegian American Line **Vistafjord** seen here in Copenhagen after she joined the Cunard fleet in 1983, she later became the **Caronia** in 1999. (Bruce Peter collection)

for economical operation thanks in part to a highly refined hull form, the project was eventually dropped as Cunard was at the time unprepared to make the huge financial outlay of replacing or augmenting the *QE2* at a time when the ship still had an anticipated service expectancy of between 10 and 15 years.

After being part of the Trafalgar House conglomerate since 1971, itself later absorbed into the Norwegian-based Kvaerner Group, the Cunard Line changed hands again in May 1998, becoming a child of its present parent, Carnival Corporation. The venerable 158-year-old line finally found itself within the fold of an organisation solidly focused on expansion of its core passenger shipping business, ready and willing to bring the line forward into the dawning 21st century. No new ship had been designed and built for Cunard since the *QE2* had made her debut in 1969, with the *Cunard Adventurer* and *Cunard Ambassador* and the later *Cunard Countess* and *Cunard Princess* having been taken over from the failed ventures of other owners while already under construction. Over the years other ships such as the former Norwegian America Line *Sagafjord* and *Vistafjord*, were acquired for cruising under the Cunard house flag, though to all intents and purposes the line had become something of a one-ship operation with none of these coming anywhere close to *QE2*'s size and performance, let alone her prestige and iconic status.

Right: The **Queen Elizabeth 2** *in the latter years of her career, with a larger funnel in traditional Cunard colours, her superstructure front modified, veranda cabins added, and her decks extended aft. (Miles Cowsill)*

CHAPTER 2

PROJECT QUEEN MARY

CUNARD

QUEEN MARY 2

Rather than trying to revive anything from 'Q5', Carnival opted instead to do its own study. The *Queen Elizabeth 2* had shown the traditional North Atlantic trade, started by Samuel Cunard in 1840, was still a viable niche passenger market at the dawning of the 21st century. Code-named 'Project Queen Mary', in recognition of Cunard's original *Queen Mary*, the purpose of the study was to determine what type of ship could be built and operated economically for a dual cruising and North Atlantic role that would be sustainable onwards as far as 40 years into the new millennium. Remarkably, the original *Queen Mary* is still considered by many to be the most successful North Atlantic ship ever built despite the dual-role *QE2*'s great popularity.[11]

'Project Queen Mary' was announced on 8th June 1998, only a week after Carnival had completed its purchase of Cunard, clearly showing the new parent's earnest intent to bring the line forward into the modern era of luxury ocean travel for half the year and express North Atlantic service for the other half, and at long last to actually BUILD! Carnival Chairman Mickey Arison later said that "we would not have bought Cunard if the concept of *Queen Mary 2* had not come along."[12] Indeed the Cunard Line had at long last ended up in the right hands.

The 'Project Queen Mary' team was headed by Stephen Payne as chief naval architect with Gerry Ellis from the Line's Miami head office being brought in to add the value of his own sea experience as a master mariner and operational expertise as the senior Cunard representative in his role as Director of Newbuilding. The existing *QE2* was itself chosen as the logical starting point for planning a new ship in the larger Vista-class size range, though with the structural stamina and higher speed needed for the six-day Southampton-New York line service. An initial conception of the proposed new ship at first announced that it would

Above: An artist rendering of the new 'Project Queen Mary' ship showing an early concept of the arrangement with only two strata of veranda cabins below the Deck 7 open promenade. (Author's collection)

be "the grandest and largest liner ever built...that will be the very pinnacle of the shipbuilder's art; the realisation of a dream of another time..."[13]

This in effect referenced Carnival's earlier 'Pinnacle Project' aimed at creating a highly prestigious elite cruise brand of its own, and that was to ultimately be achieved instead through the Cunard acquisition. As with the already abandoned 'Q5' project, this also was thought to be too elitist. It was almost a case of history being repeated, in the same way as when the 'Q3' was scrapped on the drawing boards 40 years earlier as being the wrong ship and was replaced by the more flexible 'Q4', eventually completed as the *Queen Elizabeth 2*. In the case of 'Project Queen Mary', it was eventually realised that, as a true liner, the new Cunard ship would have to provide a wide range of accommodation categories from smaller inside cabins to large duplex veranda suites for those wishing to travel at various price ranges as they did in the old 'Queens' and *QE2*.

Virtually a whole human generation had passed since the *QE2* and *Hamburg* were completed in 1969 and the *Vistafjord* four years later as the last true North Atlantic liners. Unlike a cruise ship that might make two Atlantic

Top: A cut-away illustration showing one of the **Queen Mary 2***'s ultra-deluxe duplex suites with an upper-storey bedroom and double-height private solarium. (Author's collection)*

Above: An architectural rendering from Tillberg Design of the Commodore Club lounge, designed as a modern adaptation of the forward-facing cocktail bars aboard the old Cunard 'Queens'. (Author's collection)

crossings a year as seasonal positioning voyages, a ship in the *QE2*'s transatlantic role would have to be built to structurally withstand regular service on the North Atlantic with gale-force winds of as much as 100 miles per hour, long swells measuring 150 metres (about half a liner's waterline length) from trough to trough, and 15-metre waves high enough to break over the bow deck and superstructure front at effective speeds of 45 miles per hour, or as Gerry Ellis pointed out, even with the force to cave in solid steel gangway doors in the ship's sides.[14] In other words, a liner has to maintain a precise schedule on a given route between two points, 'come hell and high water', with no option to alter the itinerary, as can a cruise ship, to evade storms, high winds and heavy seas. Things like this were a rude awakening to designers and shipyard people who had spent more than 20 years only building ships for fair-weather cruising in tropical waters.

There was also a general culture shock among Cunard's own people, both ashore and at sea, that the line might actually move forward beyond the *QE2* after some three decades with virtually no prospects of fleet growth. Most were even unaware of the ultimately cancelled 'Q5' project. At first many wondered even if it would be possible to carry on the great transatlantic tradition of express liners such as the *Normandie*, Cunard's original 'Queens', or for that matter the *QE2* still thought to be the last great liner of her genre considering the obviously enormous cost of building a unique one-off ship of this type to serve so specialised a niche market.

Stephen Payne meanwhile insisted that, rather than being created merely as a cruise ship with additional structural stamina and speed for seasonal North Atlantic service, the new 'Project Queen Mary' ship absolutely had to be designed and built structurally, first as a true ocean liner, and only then as a cruise ship. At the same time the

A portside elevation diagram of the **Queen Mary 2** *as built, with the public rooms lowered by one deck to provide an additional veranda accommodation level between these and the Deck 7 promenade above. (Chantiers de l'Atlantique)*

accommodations and passenger amenities would, as was done with the *QE2*, have to be designed first in response to the requirements of cruising, where the new ship would spend half to two-thirds of her time, and only secondarily to meet the special considerations of Atlantic service and other long sea passages.

For the purposes of 'Project Queen Mary', it was first necessary to determine the key design differences between a cruise ship and a true ocean liner. Essentially the liner would need to have a relatively deep draft and refined hull form for good stability and seakeeping during sustained high-speed sailing in deep waters. The liner would need the power to cover longer sea passages at higher speeds than normally needed for cruise service, reserve power to make up for lost headway due to fog, gales and heavy seas and the structural stamina to withstand North Atlantic sailing conditions as comfortably as possible. In response to the higher levels of on-board activity and service expected by today's cruise passengers, the liner would need to offer a

greater range of public rooms, dining and entertainment options, and other service amenities over longer periods of time at sea without port calls than are usual even in around-the-world voyages and other longer cruises. As North Atlantic sailings by their nature of offering travel from one point to another tend to attract a wider diversity of passengers, the on-board experience would also need to offer a diversity of service at least rooted in multiple-class operation, even without necessarily being promoted as such.[15]

Where the new 'Project Queen Mary' ship would, however, differ from her predecessors such as French Line's *Normandie*, the old Cunard 'Queens' and modern trendsetting liners with provision for alternative cruising roles such as the *Rotterdam*, *Oriana*, *Canberra*, *France*, *Eugenio C* and finally the *QE2*, was that there would be no provision for passengers to take their own cars or carry large amounts of checked hold baggage. Consideration also had to be given as to whether other special liner-era facilities such as

*Top: The **Queen Mary 2** was 'block built' in a dry-dock, with large items of machinery such as this Wärtsilä diesel generator set placed in the engine room before the upper hull blocks are assembled above. (Cunard)*

Above: At a later building stage a three-deck high forward superstructure block enclosing the navigating bridge, Atlantic Room and the four forward deluxe Royal Suites is lifted into position. (Cunard)

dog kennels and chilled storage rooms for ladies' fur coats would be unnecessary in the dawning new 21st century era of transatlantic travel where the choice of a sea crossing is more likely to be a discretionary preference than a matter of inescapable necessity.

Perhaps above all else was the consideration that any new Atlantic liner built for Cunard would be expected to be a worthy fleet mate and ultimate successor to the *QE2* with at least some semblance of her distinctive character and iconic aura of singularity. Design of the new 'Project Queen Mary' ship thus started with a detailed review of the *QE2*'s plans, with her overall hull dimensions, passenger capacity and speed taken as being ideal for the new ship. The *QE2*'s length and draft were already known to work well within the constraints of the swinging basin and passenger terminal facilities at Southampton's Eastern Docks and the thousand-foot-long finger piers then still being used by Cunard at the Port of New York's Consolidated Passenger Terminals. The ship's height above the water would be restricted to 62 metres for passage under the Verrazano Narrows Bridge at the entrance to New York City's harbours, though otherwise a moderate increase in length was possible and the beam could also be increased for a larger ship if needed.[16] Given the *QE2*'s dimensions a modern Panamax-max ship of the Holland America Vista class with a measure of around 90,000 tons was at first thought possible, and desirable for being able to sail through the Panama Canal on cruises.

Although the *QE2* offered a very wide range of accommodations, ranging from small inside single-berth rooms through various hotel-style standard-grade cabins to the veranda accommodations, including split-level and duplex two-storey suites added during various refits, the overall accommodation standard throughout the cruise industry had risen greatly, with the latest world-class cruise ships offering considerably greater average room sizes and a predominance of rooms with verandas. A new ship of the *QE2*'s size, or for that matter even in the larger Vista-class league, with a refined hull form, powerful propulsion plant and the diversity of on-board amenities for express Atlantic service would be left with a reduced capacity for revenue-earning passenger accommodations.

Since the *QE2* only ever made a single passage of the Panama Canal each year as part of her around-the-world cruise, the decision was made in favour of sailing instead 'around the Horn' with an altogether larger ship having a volumetric measure of around 150,000 tons. With a planned overall length of 350 metres, a beam increased to 40 metres and the *QE2*'s 10-metre draft retained, this would provide the stability for building the ship almost entirely of steel and avoiding the technical problems of complicated bi-metallic joints in the exterior shell. The new ship's considerably greater size would accommodate around 2,600 passengers in lower berths, against the *QE2*'s total passenger head count (including upper berths) of 2,025 and the spacious Vista-class *Zuiderdam*'s 1,848 double-occupancy figure. Surpassing the 137,000-ton measure of Royal Caribbean's *Voyager of the Seas*, this would once again give Cunard, for a while at least, the great prestige of having the world's largest liner.

The *QE2*'s passenger accommodations, public amenities and deck spaces were also reviewed to determine which aspects of these contributed most to her enduring success and should be brought forward to the new ship and which needed to be modified, rethought and reworked to reflect newer developments in cruise ship design through the more than 30 years since the *QE2* was built. Spaces such as the Queens Room, Midships and Chart Room Bars, Golden Lion Pub and the main restaurants with their full height windows overlooking the sea and the exclusive Queens and

Above: At an earlier stage of building, fabrication of the hull proceeds forward towards the bow, which will be assembled above its bulbous forefoot already in place at the bottom of the picture. (Cunard)

Above: With some of her lifeboat davits still empty, superstructure and interior work yet to be completed, the **Queen Mary 2** *manoeuvres into the Loire Estuary with the precautionary aid of tugs as she undertakes her first sea trials on 25th September 2003. (Cunard)*

Princess Grills, that had become signature Cunard shipboard institutions, were tick marked to be retained and redeveloped. The Grand Lounge, originally the Double Room, since then reworked and reconstituted numerous times in a never wholly successful attempt to create a show lounge was crossed off as needing to be entirely replaced by a proper theatre with full-production stage, raked orchestra and dress-circle seating. Likewise, most of the accommodations, with their wide variety of complex interlocking cabin layouts and numerous secondary passages on Five and Six Decks, were crossed off as needing to be completely redesigned on the modern cruise-ship basis of a greatly simplified layout with a predominance of cabins and suites, each with their own individual private verandas. This alone would result in a significant change in overall plan from anything that had ever been done for any North Atlantic express liner.

Looking at newer cruise-industry developments, and

particularly at Carnival's own upscale Holland America Vista class, the 'Project Queen Mary' plan was also rounded out with ample alternative dining venues and a heightened emphasis on health and fitness amenities. Also looking back to the grand-luxe era of ocean travel, Cunard wanted to reintroduce the idea of the winter garden lounge as a pleasant and more passive traditional place for passengers to pass the hours during Atlantic crossings and other longer sea passages.

Five leading European shipyards, Alsthom Chantiers de l'Atlantique, Harland & Wolff, Howaldtswerke-Deutsche Werft, Kvaerner Masa Yards and Meyer Werft tendered their bids to build the new Cunard 'Queen'. During the annual SeaTrade conference and trade show at Miami in March 2000 it was announced that a letter of agreement had been signed with the Chantiers de l'Atlantique shipyard at Saint-Nazaire in France's Pays de la Loire region. Although Carnival had worked extensively with Fincantieri, which had already built most of the Group's new ships, including the *Zuiderdam*, then being completed as the first of Holland America's ultra-spacious 90,000-ton ships of the new Vista class, the Italian builders were unable to tender for the building as both their Marghera and Monfalcone yards were fully booked building other large cruise ships, mainly for Carnival.

Final competition for the order had been between the French yard and the Belfast Harland & Wolff yard. While there was strong sentiment in favour of this great new Cunard ocean liner of the 21st century being built in the United Kingdom, the stark reality of today's highly globalised passenger shipping industry was that Cunard, with its own headquarters then located in Miami, was itself no longer British, having become part of a publicly held Carnival Corporation also based in the United States. While Carnival's management was sympathetic to the cause of

Top: Completed and officially handed over to Cunard, the **Queen Mary 2** *leaves her birthplace in Saint-Nazaire and heads out to sea on 22nd December 2003. (Cunard)*

Above: The **Queen Mary 2** *alongside in the Chantiers de l'Atlantique's 'Forme C' dock at night immediately prior to her delivery and departure from France.*

*Above: The Grand Lobby showing one of the curved processional staircases and John McKenna's **Queen Mary**-inspired bas-relief North Atlantic sculpture at upper left. (Cunard)*

Harland & Wolff's very survival being contingent on securing the 'Project Queen Mary' building contract and to the importance to Belfast's people, they ultimately ended up favouring Chantiers de l'Atlantique's bid on the basis of the yard's proven recent experiences in building large and sophisticated new cruise ships and in their greater resources to finance the building of so expensive a ship.

When the Compagnie Générale Transatlantique (later more universally known simply as the French Line) first started building iron-hulled paddle steamers for their own mail and passenger services to New York and Central America, half of these were constructed at Greenock by Scott's Shipbuilding & Engineering with the other half required by law to be constructed in France. There were at the time no French shipyards with the capacity to build the larger and more powerful steamers needed for the emerging transatlantic steamer trade. Thus the original Chantiers de l'Atlantique yard established in 1861 at Penhoët on the north bank of the Loire estuary was founded by John Scott to build exclusively for the then newly founded French Line. During the time of his contract to start up the new French yard, Scott also recruited and trained a skilled local workforce to build ships in France.

The yard flourished, eventually merging with its competitors from the region and broadening its scope to take on other building work for the French navy and for various other shipping lines, both at home in France and overseas. The yard retained its original role as virtually the house shipwrights to the French Line and as a leading passenger ship builder for the French nation itself. From the Loire Estuary have come such significant ships as French Line's art deco *Ile de France*, the incomparable *Normandie* and the elite modern *France*, as well as the lesser-known Compagnie de Navigation Sudatlantique liners *l'Atlantique* and *Pasteur*, that despite their short careers

*Above: The Queen's and Princess Grill restaurants that exclusively serve occupants of the **Queen Mary 2's** top-grade accommodations offer panoramic views to either side of the ship and aft, as did the original grill restaurant aboard the old **Queen Mary**. (Cunard)*

under the tricolour were in their own right nonetheless significant developments in the shipbuilders art.

Following the 1960s completions of ships such as the *France* and *Queen Elizabeth 2* at the conclusion of the traditional liner era, a new wave of progressively larger and more sophisticated cruise ships have set the pace for the current leisure passenger shipping era. Reconstituted as Alstom Chantiers de l'Atlantique, the company diversified into the building of supertankers and other specialised ships. It also entered a new era of passenger cruising with ships such as the Holland America *Nieuw Amsterdam* and

Noordam completed in the early 1980s and Royal Caribbean's *Sovereign of the Seas*, the first new ship to surpass the former *France*'s measure after being converted for full-time cruising as the *Norway*. Along with later ships of the *Sovereign of the Seas* and higher capacity *Legend of the Seas* classes, *Star Princess*, the exclusive eight-ship Renaissance *R* series and at about the time of signing the letter of agreement for Cunard's 'Project Queen Mary', the first of three large Panamax-max *Millennium*-class ships for Celebrity Cruises.

At a time when Britain seemed to lack the capacity to

The vast 1,347-seat Britannia main restaurant showing artist Barbara Broekman's tapestry depicting a mythical Cunard liner departing from New York. (Cunard)

The Commodore Club's bar with its 1:100 scale illuminated model of the ship commissioned from the Dutch model maker Henrik Brandwijk is a 21st century rendition of the forward-facing cocktail bars on the old 'Queens'. (Cunard)

*Following on from the **QE2** idea of naming her 736 Club for the ship's yard number, the **Queen Mary 2**'s G32 Club is thoughtfully located aft of the Queen's Room where late-night entertainment is least likely to disturb sleeping passengers and crew. (Cunard)*

build a new Cunard 'Queen', even if only financially so, it
seems ironic that that this great shipyard, itself founded
with the help of Scottish expertise and experience nearly
150 years earlier, should be the one to tender the winning
bid for a Cunard 'Queen' for the first time in France.
Following on other Anglo French initiatives such as the
Concorde supersonic airliner and the Eurotunnel venture,
perhaps the whole idea is less strange than it might seem,
especially given that both Great Britain and France have
long been friends, war-time allies and are now both
members of the European Union.

Concept and design

The formal building contract was signed on 6th
November 2000, when it was also announced that the new
ship's name would be *Queen Mary 2*. The first steel was cut
for her construction, starting the actual building more than
a year later on 16th January 2002. In the meantime
detailed design work with the shipyard's technical team and
the ship's interior architects was developed, along with
preparation of the working drawings and ordering of
materials, machinery and fittings, and the letting of
contracts to specialist sub contractors and turnkey suppliers.

Among the main technical issues to be dealt with at the
earliest stages of the detailed planning was that of designing
a deep-draft express North Atlantic liner hull. While this
would need a slender fore-body form at the waterline to
part the seas as gently as possible at speed so as to create
the minimum of flank turbulence along the ship's sides, it
would need the buoyancy and inherent stability to support
a massive amount of internal passenger space, both within
the hull and throughout a tall superstructure above. The
fore-body would also have to be balanced against a fairly
full stern form, needed to support four external propulsion

*Top: The Chart Room lounge, now a Cunard signature feature aboard all three of
today's 'Queens' serves the* **Queen Mary 2** *especially well, among other things, as a
daytime focus of social activity during North Atlantic crossings and other long sea
passages. (Cunard)*

*Above: The Todd English Restaurant provides an alternative dining experience
available to all passengers regardless of the accommodation grade booked. (Cunard)*

The first facility of its kind at sea, Illuminations, seen here with its projection dome raised into the ceiling, combines the function of an auditorium, cinema and fully functional planetarium. (Cunard)

pods rather than conventional propellers and rudders. No such hull had ever been built, nor had so large a ship of such high performance been built since the *QE2*, with the one exception of the smaller 20,000-ton express gas-turbine powered Baltic ferry *Finnjet*, delivered in 1977 for service between Helsinki and Travemünde. It fell to Stephen Payne and his colleagues on the 'Project Queen Mary' team, which included representatives from Fincantieri's technical department as well as those from Chantiers de l'Atlantique's design department from the time the yard became involved in the process.

With a total propulsion power of 86 mega-Watts from four Rolls Royce external self-contained propulsion pods, auxiliary power for the bow thrusters, stabilisers and other services such as air conditioning and waste processing and a 16 mega-Watt hotel load, the *Queen Mary 2* would need to generate up to 120 mega-Watts of electrical power, equivalent to the power needed for a city of Southampton's

The red-upholstered seats at the centre of Illuminations recline for viewing planetarium shows when the dome is lowered above these. (Cunard)

One of the Queen's Room galleries at the ship's sides where large windows admit plenty of daylight in this remarkably high-ceilinged space and provide a panorama of the outside world. (Cunard)

size. This would be produced by a combined aggregate of diesel and gas-turbine generator sets. The diesel generator plant alone, consisting of four Wärtsilä clean-combustion EnviroEngines, each driving a 16.8 mega-Watt generator, would produce enough power to run the ship with all its auxiliary and hotel services at the lower speeds used for cruising. The aviation-style General Electric gas turbine generator sets would provide an additional 50 mega-Watts of power to run the four propulsion pods at full bore for express transatlantic service or other long deep-sea passages made at higher speeds.

While the diesel power plant would be conventionally arranged deep within the ship's hull, the altogether lighter and more compact gas turbine units were to be located atop the superstructure in an enclosure behind the funnel. The principal reason for this was to avoid the need for large-diameter inlets and uptakes for the gas turbines having to lead down through some 15 decks to the machinery compartments below, adding to the number of casings passing through the spaces for public rooms and accommodations. This arrangement also offered the added flexibility of providing a complete and self-contained alternative power source elsewhere in the ship for use in case of the main engine room being disabled in an emergency or at times when any of the generator sets at either location would need to be serviced or repaired.

The hull design that emerged from this collaborative effort adopted a large bulbous-form underwater forefoot at the bow to provide added buoyancy and stability forward and balance the fore-body longitudinally against the greater massif of the stern that would support the four propulsion pods. As Stephen Payne likes to point out when explaining the ship to others, "It still amazes me that each one of those pods weigh 320 tons, which is the weight of a fully-loaded 747 jumbo jet at takeoff."[17] By comparison, the internal

Top: Part of the informal King's Court dining area, designed on the land-based Marché idea, where various types of cuisine are on offer through the day and evening. (Cunard)

Above: A break-out area in the Connexions University at Sea facility that can be used as needed for various educational, business and private functions. (Cunard)

Top: The two-storey entrance to the ship's Spa and other health and beauty facilities, seen here from its upper level. (Cunard)

Above: Located two decks above the Commodore Club, the slightly smaller Atlantic Room also has a forward outlook over the ship's bow. (Cunard)

electric motors fitted aboard the *QE2* during her 1986-7 re-engining each weighed 295 tons, in addition to the ship's twin 44.5-ton controllable-pitch propellers. The *QM2*'s self-contained pods would afford the added weight advantage of eliminating altogether the 80 metres propeller shafting runs, thrust blocks, enclosing bossings and stern brackets of conventional shafted propulsion, as well as completely doing away with the need for a conventional rudder and steering gear. The *QM2* is thus in effect a huge outboard motor craft, with pods beneath the stern rather than attached to the transom powerboat-style.

Experience with the few large cruise ships built with external pod propulsion at the time, including the Celebrity *Millennium*, also built at Chantiers de l'Atlantique, showed a flat transom stern to be best suited to the likewise flat underwater plane of the hull's stern. Concerned about the possible effects of 'following seas' in North Atlantic line service and other long ocean passages, Stephen Payne favoured a traditional curved cruiser stern. Here a compromise was reached by adopting a combination transom and cruiser stern of the Castanzi hull form from Costa's *Eugenio C*, completed in 1966 at Cantiere Riuniti dell Adriatico, now Fincantieri's Monfalcone yard and named after the ship's naval architect Stefano Castanzi.

While the new *QM2* was being designed for express North Atlantic service, with the need for a substantial freeboard height of the hull's sides and for the lifeboats to be carried considerably higher above the waterline than is customary with cruise ships, the ship's cruising role also called for a high proportion of cabins and suites with private verandas. In cruise ship design this is normally accomplished following the *Royal Princess* approach with a predominant hotel-block-style superstructure above a relatively low-sided hull housing the public spaces no more than three or four decks above the waterline, with the lifeboats and other safety equipment at the superstructure base directly above these. Thus, even in the case of the largest ships such as the 137,000-ton *Voyager of the Seas*, the boat deck was only some 12 metres above the sea, compared with the 24-metre height of the *QE2*'s boat deck. This was resolved by in effect extending the *QM2*'s hull height up to include the first three accommodation decks above the public rooms, with Deck 7 becoming the main promenade at a similar height of 23.94 metres. An intermediate run of public spaces was located at this level, half way up the hotel block, with the usual range of lido deck pools and other more informal daytime spaces being located topmost, above an additional four-and-a-half decks given over mainly to veranda accommodations. Outer accommodations on the upper hull Decks 4, 5 and 6 were also given verandas, though these were within smaller openings in the hull's shell plating, affording them a fairly high degree of protection from the seas. Though its rationale was different, the plan was by coincidence quite similar to the 'sandwich' layout of *Canberra* with three separate strata of public spaces atop, amidst and below her cabin decks.

The *QM2*'s planning and building as a true express North Atlantic liner called for a certain degree of flexibility in interpretation of, and even amendment to, the classification and safety rules under which she would be registered. The prevailing rules for deep-sea passenger ships in cruise service, called for lifeboats to be stowed no more than 15 metres above the waterline. Through consultation with the British Maritime & Coastguard Agency and the United States Coast Guard, a ten-metre increase in height was allowed as a 'retrograde option' to provide added protection for the boats in severe North Atlantic sea conditions. Another special situation arose with fire safety requirements for sprinkler heads being required

Top & Above: Two views of the Winter Garden, with its floral carpeting and upholstery, artificial potted trees and painted trompe l'oeil effect plaster ceiling, endeavours to recreate the essence of traditional liner era or perhaps London's Kew Gardens. (Cunard)

Top: Honouring the Line's founder, Sir Samuel's was created as a wine bar, though it serves well also as an aperitif bar thanks to its location near the Britannia Restaurant. (Cunard)

Above: The ladies hairdressing salon forms part of the **Queen Mary 2's** *extensive health and beauty complex located at the forward end of the promenade deck. (Cunard)*

inside the ship's planetarium dome, a situation that had never before arisen in the design of a ship. There was no apparent provision in the rules for the exemption of an overhead projection surface such as this from being fractured by the need for these devices. A compromise was at first found by the alternative use of a water cannon with sufficient throw range to douse the area beneath the dome, though ultimately its projection surface was made of a white porous material that was penetrable from sprinklers attached to the steel deckhead above.[18]

Before the final building costs for *QM2* could be set and a contract signed with the yard an 11-metre exact scale model of the hull was made and rigorously tested at the Maritime Research Institute Netherlands (MARIN) in the Dutch town of Wageningen near Arnhem. Apart from showing how well the overall hull form would work under various sea conditions the ship could be expected to encounter, the tests were also vitally important to determine the optimum location and arrangement of the four external propulsion pods that would propel the ship at continuous speeds of up to 29 knots in line service on the North Atlantic.

The model tank testing done at MARIN showed that the hull would have excellent sea-keeping characteristics and that its slender waterline form at the bow would part the waters with ease, even in heavy seas. It also showed that the four movable-fin stabilisers served well to suppress rolling and maintain an on-board comfort level already determined from service experience with the *QE2*. Various arrangements of the propulsion pods were tried, with the best results achieved from an arrangement of two azimuthing (turnable) pods aft of the two fixed pods some 30 metres further forward and at a greater distance outwards from the hull's centreline. A centreline rudder was also tried and eventually eliminated.

Inspired by the famous Hollywood Bowl band shell in Los Angeles, California, the Queen's Room is an updated adaptation of its popular earlier namesake introduced aboard the **QE2** *in 1969. (Cunard)*

After the building contract was signed, the yard's technical team proposed some modifications to the hull form with slightly increased overall dimensions and a higher displacement. A second model was made and tested at MARIN, from which a final hull line emerged for the ship as built.

From the earliest design concept stages of 'Project Queen Mary', long before Chantiers de l'Atlantique became involved, Cunard had already decided to adopt some of the compelling key design features of French Line's legendary *Normandie* that, upon her spectacular 1935 debut, had created the 80,000-ton liner mystique that had set the pace for the original Cunard 'Queens'. As Stephen Payne had pointed out in a paper he prepared for the Royal Institution of Naval Architects, the *Normandie* was designed around a remarkable axial plan, with passenger circulation among its many open-plan and airy public spaces being by way of wide thoroughfares along the ship's centreline

Top: The Queen's Room seen here with the monogrammed stage curtain in place. (Cunard)

Above: The Illuminations auditorium with its retractable planetarium dome lowered for a celestial show. (Cunard)

making the whole plan amazingly intuitive and straightforward for those onboard. The boiler and engine-room casings, ventilation and hold access shafts, all stairways, lifts and other vertical services were parted to either side of a broad right of way running fore and aft, dead-centre along the middle of each deck.

Axial plans of this sort had been successfully tried as far back as 1914, when introduced on a large scale aboard the Cunard Line *Aquitania*'s Hamburg America Line rival *Vaterland* and again in 1929-30 in the North German Lloyd Blue Riband record breakers *Bremen* and *Europa*. With the increase in size from the approximately 50,000-ton scale of these to approximately 80,000 tons the *Normandie*'s significantly increased sense of spaciousness, along with a newfound sense of shipboard informality and the typically French sense of *grand gesture* made the whole approach infinitely more appealing. This, together with an extensive use of decorative glasswork and innovative architectural lighting caused the *Normandie* to be nicknamed in some quarters as 'the ship of light'. When the *Queen Mary* made her debut a year later her plan, arranged around a central arrangement of vertical accesses and other services, was seen as being altogether more traditional, despite the fact that on average she offered a higher grade of cabin accommodations with a greater proportion of larger hotel-style rooms.

At around 150,000 tons the new 'Queen Mary' would undoubtedly be large enough to carry off a *Normandie*-style axial plan with equal, if not even greater, aplomb. As the main suites of public rooms would be located cruise-ship style within the hull decks, the plan would benefit from the new liner's full width of 41 metres without the rooms being flanked on their outer sides by the promenade decks, as was done aboard the *Normandie*. As part of a bid to locate the *Queen Mary 2*'s promenade deck and lifeboats at QE2-height above the waterline, Decks 2 and 3, where the main public spaces were to be located, were each to have a design height of 4.5 metres, somewhat greater than the usual single-height headroom space of 3.5 to 3.8 metres in most modern passenger ships. Double-height spaces such as the main dining room and show lounge would be nearly nine metres, asserting the same sense of open spaciousness as the *Normandie*'s celebrated triple-height *Grand Salle à Manger*, *Grand Salon*, *Fumoir* and their related circulating spaces.

The new HAPAG-Lloyd cruise ship *Europa* had been completed in 1999 with a then unprecedented design height in modern passenger shipbuilding of 4.5 metres throughout her entire main suite of public rooms.[19] This was done as a means of recreating the sense of elegance and spaciousness of earlier liners, where it was customary for the ceiling height of the promenade deck rooms to be extended up through the boat deck level above, partly to attain the added headroom then thought to be necessary for larger public spaces, and also to raise the boat deck accommodations above the lifeboat line to avoid obstructing the view from these rooms. In the case of the new *Europa*, however, the public deck was beneath the accommodation block on the uppermost hull deck.

Tillberg Design, their British partners, SMC Design, along with the London-based firm, designteam, were brought into the 'Project Queen Mary' team at an early stage to handle the ship's architectural design and interior decoration. As this ship was being built entirely as a private venture without government loan guarantees, there would be no questions asked in Parliament about the interior designers and their work, no involvement of National design councils and no professional lobbying as there had been during the *QE2*'s planning. Through some three decades of service, countless refits, reconfigurations, modernisations and refurbishments the *QE2* had taken on

Top: A view from the upper gallery of the G32 Club, arranged somewhat like the terraced afterdecks of a ship. (Cunard)

*Above: Given pride of place overlooking the bow, the **Queen Mary 2**'s library has one of the world's largest ocean-going collections of books and media. (Cunard)*

Top: The library with its forward view, easy chairs, display tables and other features is an inviting place to spend a while during days at sea. (Cunard)

*Above: A signature Cunard feature since the **QE2**'s Project Lifestyle refit in the 1990s, the Golden Lion Pub is a modern ocean-going adaptation of the British Public House. (Cunard)*

the warm, welcoming, intimately friendly and comfortable club-like atmosphere of a favoured urban hotel with a devoted loyal following. The initial élan of her original sixties modernity and the 'wow' of other features added over the years was never overstated or *de trop*, but rather welcoming and inviting, yielding right away to the sense of comfort and well being that has perhaps always been the *QE2*'s best selling point.

The architectural and decorative approach for the *QM2* was that those most endearing and enduring features of the *QE2* were to influence the new ship's design with entirely new things rather than themselves being copied or replicated per se. Ocean liner eclecticism, art deco revival and other forms of pastiche were to be avoided in favour of what Tomas Tillberg, Robert's son and head of the firm's Fort Lauderdale office described as a "a new shipboard architecture."[20] The designers were called on rather to take a similarly luxurious contemporary international hotelier style that Dennis Lennon and Partners had achieved aboard the *QE2* three decades earlier that would reflect rather the richer interpretation of today's best landside hospitality and ocean-going cruise ship design.

A *Heritage Trail* illustrating Cunard's history introduced aboard the *QE2* during the 1990s was to be brought forward and in effect more closely woven into the fabric of the new ship's design. Other hallmark features of the earlier Cunarder such as her Queens Room, Chart Room bar and multi-purpose Yacht Club were to be given an entirely new interpretation rather than being merely reproduced. For instance there would be no glass fibre backlit latticed ceiling and inverted trumpet columns of the old Queens Room, but rather a new Hollywood Bowl-inspired theme for its interpretation for the *QM2* to set the mood for elegant afternoon teas, pre-dinner concerts and 'black and white' evening balls. The pub was to assert the

The Britannia Restaurant's impressive central nave, reaches a height of nearly 12 metres from the floor to its illuminated glass dome above. (Cunard)

61

Top: The **Queen Mary 2***'s Mayfair Shops uphold a trend started by Cunard in 1936 of offering a diverse selection of merchandise for sale on board the Line's 'Queens'. (Cunard)*

Above: Children too are well provided for with their own public spaces such as this playroom with its own adjacent deck area. (Cunard)

feel of this uniquely British institution without resorting to ersatz Tudor countryside rusticity but rather in the sense of today's lifestyles with an added nautical touch. As Andy Collier, project manager of the Tillberg Design/SMC Design team put it: "the new ship's design offers a 'tip of the hat' to tradition without itself setting a retrospective mood in its own right."[21]

As well-experienced and diversified professionals in the modern passenger ship design field, the greatest challenge they faced was to identify and adapt the essence of those most desirable liner-era features of ships such as the *Normandie* and the old Cunard 'Queens' to contemporary shipboard living for the 21st century. At a very early stage of planning, Robert Tillberg, his firm's by then semi-retired senior partner, had visualised broad high-ceilinged axial 'Walkways' extending through the public decks, with larger spaces such as the restaurants and show lounges at their ends and other rooms to either side.

Research of traditional liner design done by Tillberg's office at Viken, near Helsingborg in Sweden showed that, rather than the *Normandie* herself, Compagnie de Navigation Sudatlantique's liner *l'Atlantique* was perhaps a more suitable reference for the new Cunard ship. The smaller 40,000-ton *l'Atlantique*'s axial plan was in fact better articulated and more cohesive, with the main restaurant included in the ship's upper-decks main suite of public spaces designed for tropical service to the eastern seaboard of South America. Her three principal public spaces included the rectangular restaurant and main lounge along with an attractive colonnaded *Salon Ovale*, serving as a ballroom in its own right, but also as an access to other smaller spaces such as the chapel and two private salons at its diagonal extremities. Tillberg Design developed an enlarged and elongated rendition of this plan for Decks 2 and 3 aboard the *QM2*, adopting the *Salon Ovale* as a

Churchill's Cigar Lounge, adjacent to the Commodore Club, is the modern-day successor to the shipboard smoking room, where one can still enjoy a good smoke. (Cunard)

This pleasant seating area near the health and beauty facilities is yet another informal gathering space adding to the diversity of places passengers can enjoy on Atlantic crossings and longer cruises. (Cunard)

connecting atrium space amidships, the main lounge and
restaurant forward- and aft-most, and with other spaces
such as the Cunard signature Midships Bar, Chart Room
and Golden Lion Pub opening out from the oval atrium
space and the central walkways from Robert Tillberg's
original proposals.[22]

As there was already a vast amount of open public space
within the hull, including at least four enormous double-
height rooms, Stephen Payne was reluctant to agree also to
a large cruise-ship style atrium extending up through the
structural strength decks above. He favoured instead
designing the central *Salon Ovale* space rather as an elegant
hotel-style lobby modelled on the entrance hall of Eltham
Palace, the home built for Stephen Courtauld and his family
near London in the 1930s. This modern country house,
that incorporated the remaining Great Hall from the
medieval royal palace built at Eltham in the 15th century,
featured as its centrepiece a spectacular entrance hall
designed by the Swedish architect Rolf Engströmer that has
since become a veritable icon of contemporary 20th century
architecture. Panelled in dark Australian blackbean veneer
inlaid with marquetry work depicting Italian and
Scandinavian scenes, the round cornered triangular space
was of a suitable scale for adaptation as a shipboard lobby in
the style of *L'Atlantique*'s *Salon Ovale* already envisaged by
Tillberg.

Stephen Payne was himself familiar with Eltham Palace
as it was near his own home and he had visited it a number
of times. Now a holding of English Heritage and open to
the public, the house remains as a surviving example of the
thirties-era ocean liner styling that influenced its design and
decoration. Stephen brought members of the 'Project
Queen Mary' design team, including Andy Collier and his
colleagues from SMC Design to the property, convincing
them that, perhaps a single-height space such as this on

Top: The Balmoral Suite's spacious living and dining area, with the double-height solarium area in the background and stairs to the upper level bedroom at the right (Cunard)

Above: Living and dining space within the curved superstructure front in the Queen Mary Suite, which can be combined by way of the doors in the background with the adjoining Queen Anne Suite. (Cunard)

A partial view of the duplex Holyrood Suite's main-level living and dining areas showing details of the furnishings and fittings. (Cunard)

Deck 3 would have sufficient impact that a larger atrium would be unnecessary. Deck 3 was chosen as the embarkation point as its height above sea level and location relative to the bow corresponded approximately with that of the *QE2*'s circular Midships Lobby on Two Deck and existing boarding bridge arrangements at the Southampton and New York terminals to be used by both ships. Ultimately, Cunard's marketing people convinced the designers that passengers would expect a larger and more spectacular open space, and the Grand Lobby, as it was named, was extended up through the three accommodation decks above.[23]

Another special concern of the *QM2*'s design was the question of providing direct access to her greater than usual number of full width public rooms. In addition to the Britannia main restaurant and principal entertainment venue, the Royal Court Theatre, the Queens Room and a second large theatre-style auditorium were also to extend across the ship's full beam. Early concepts of the layout called for the Queens Room located aft on the Promenade deck. As the plan was developed and refined, it was decided to also locate these large spaces within the high-ceilinged realm of Decks 2 and 3. Access to the added spaces fully aft and forward on these decks was ingeniously arranged by way of galleries at the ship's sides bypassing the Britannia Restaurant and Royal Court Theatre at an intermediate level between Decks 2 and 3, called Deck 3L (3 Lower). Resembling the enclosed Quarter and Upper Deck circulating promenades aboard the *QE2*, with full-height windows overlooking the sea along their outer sides, these were in effect nested behind the Royal Court's terraced 'dress circle' seating and tucked in between the Britannia's main and mezzanine levels in such a way that their existence was unapparent from within either of these rooms.

Top: The duplex Holyrood Suite's upper level looking into the bedoom from the stairway and solarium gallery. (Cunard)

Above: A standard-grade veranda cabin on one of the upper decks above the lifeboats. (Cunard)

65

Aft, the Queens Room was rooted slightly below Deck 3 level above the main galleys on Deck 2 and the G32 Discotheque (taking its name from the ship's yard number) brought further down to Deck 3L level. The forward galleries were ramped up to Deck 3 level where they form a loop around the double-height Illuminations auditorium, arranged with the ConnXions shipboard college at sea and conferencing facilities tucked in beneath its steeply inclined main-level seating. Forward most, within the converging lines of the ship's bow, Deck 3 also housed a block of 41 crew and staff cabins.

The Illuminations space was originally conceived as being a general-purpose auditorium and cinema serving as an alternative large-capacity entertainment venue. Cunard wanted to offer some sort of special attraction that would be unique to the *QM2*, and that would give passengers a memorable experience as part of their overall experience of the ship. After considering various possibilities the 'Project Queen Mary' design team decided that, based on the popularity of the London Planetarium as a tourist attraction in the British Capital, an ocean-going facility of its kind would offer just such an experience in a fully functional space that would work well within the scale of a ship. Yet something of this type would be too specialised to have a dedicated space of its own without also being usable for different purposes outside the hours of its use as a planetarium.

The solution was to fit a retractable projection dome above the Illuminations' central seating area. The dome's crown was fixed within a centreline casing extending up through the accommodation deck above, and fitted with two moveable rim sections that could be extended downwards like the ailerons of an aircraft wing to form an apparently seamless and absolutely perfectly hemispherical projection surface for celestial, Imax and other special film shows. Of the auditorium's 473 seats, the 170 of those located directly beneath the dome and upholstered in gold are fitted with release mechanisms that allow them to tilt back for viewing planetarium features.

Six Sky-Cam projectors are located in this part of the room and controlled from an elaborate projection booth that is also equipped for Imax, various digital and video formats for presentation on the auditorium's large plasma screens, as well as twin 35mm film projectors for feature motion picture screenings. Where film showings aboard many cruise ships are now relegated to the distribution of lower-quality digital and video material via the cabin TV systems, the *QM2* was equipped to uphold the *QE2*'s superbly unmatched standard of true cinema-quality motion picture screenings.

Illuminations, together with the 1,096-seat Royal Court Theatre, with its sectioned revolving stage, orchestra pit and full-scale fly-over tower for theatrical scenery changes were designed and equipped to offer the *QM2*'s passengers entertainment facilities rivalling any of the best play houses and cinemas of New York's Broadway or London's West End. Along with the Golden Lion Pub, Sir Samuel's wine bar, the Chart Room, Midships Bar and a wide variety of alternate restaurants and other diversions, the *QM2* was set to offer a 'night on the town' experience just about the equal of anything either of these two cities has to offer in a totally safe and self-contained setting. In total the milieu of the *QM2*'s Deck 2 and 3 facilities was of unprecedented diversity at the time the ship was planned and built, and continues to retain its special sense of sophistication even despite the debut of several larger cruise ships since then.

The Deck 7 public spaces at the boat deck level include the Winter Garden and a King's Court, a large open-plan informal and largely al fresco dining area, both of which together also can serve as lifeboat mustering areas for

The spacious Deck 7 promenade looking aft on port side showing the lifeboats and the large multi-point davits that swing them out over the deck rail for lowering. (Miles Cowsill)

A close-up look at the **Queen Mary 2's** side showing the cabin verandas which are open above the lifeboats and protected behind smaller openings in the hull's shell plating below. (Miles Cowsill)

68

*A view along the **Queen Mary 2**'s starboard side as seen from the open observation space forward on Deck 11 directly below the navigating bridge. (Miles Cowsill)*

*The **Queen Mary 2**'s fully enclosed navigating bridge has the same distinctive dark-framed window inset as the **QE2** and is likewise floated above an open forward viewing gallery on the deck beneath it. (Miles Cowsill)*

passengers in the case of an emergency. These spaces were bracketed, forward by the extensive health spa facilities forward, and by the exclusive Princess and Queen's Grill Restaurants aft for the exclusive use of those occupying the ship's top-grade suites and cabins. The pinnacle Queen's Grill was also adjoined by its own Queen's Grill Lounge, as an aperitif bar and private club room for occupants of the elite among the elite. The Deck 7 public rooms were completely encircled by a wide promenade deck beneath the lifeboats and excursion launches. The deck is wide enough to also accommodate deckchairs without compromising its all-important function as the lifeboat embarkation platform in the event of an emergency. At its forward end the promenade passes within the curved superstructure front in a very much liner-reminiscent manner where it overlooks the ship's forward decks and bow.

Above this level, the Library and Commodore Club lounge were located forward on Decks 8 and 9, where they have large windows in the superstructure front and a commanding view forward over the ship's bow. The Commodore Club was created as a modern rendition of the semi-circular forward cocktail lounges that were an immensely popular feature of the old Cunard 'Queens'. While the *Queen Mary*'s cocktail lounge was always a cabin class space, the corresponding room aboard the *Queen Elizabeth* ended up later in her second-class domain following reallocation of some of the ship's public areas later in her career. Directly below her bridge, the *QM2* sports a delightful open deck space, a wonderful place for watching port arrivals and other points of interest, that follows the curvilinear form of the superstructure front, passing beneath the ship's enclosed bridge wings at either side in a fashion similar to corresponding deck spaces on the original 'Queens'. Overlooking this deck is the Atlantic Room that

Top: The **Queen Mary 2**'*s afterdecks retain the liner appearance of those on the* **QE2**, *especially with regard to the use of streamlined wind-screening to either side. (Miles Cowsill)*

Above: : Likewise the forward observation deck beneath the navigating bridge is also a throwback to the **QE2**, *and even further back to the old* '**Queens'**. *(Miles Cowsill)*

The unmistakably nautical milieu of white-painted steel, teak deck covering and glass sets the mood for the promenade's passage around the superstructure front's inner side. (Miles Cowsill)

serves as an informal sheltered observation room. Above this room a viewing gallery was included with windows overlooking the workings of the navigating bridge, though this has never been opened to passengers, no doubt as a security concern.

Designed as a true liner, the *QM2* was given a longer bow deck and more gradually terraced afterdecks similar to the *QE2*'s original profile to diminish the wind resistance and sailplane effects of the more dominant cruise-ship superstructure forms to which we have all now become accustomed. This in turn has made possible a *QE2*-style arrangement of pool and lido decks aft, principally at Deck 7 and 8 levels. A swimming pool, whirlpool baths, lido, café, and adjacent recreational facilities were also located atop the superstructure beneath a retractable glass roof comprising the Pavilion Pool ahead of the funnel as a central focus of the uppermost stratum of public spaces.

The *Queen Mary 2* was built with lower-berth accommodations for 2,620 passengers in 1,310 cabins and suites, and a maximum total of 3,090 souls with all upper Pullman berths, settee beds and baby cots occupied. The design and outfitting of all standard-grade cabins generally follows that of Carnival's Vista-class Holland America ships. But for a Cunard 'Queen', the top deluxe Queen's Grill category suites would have to be something remarkably special, and so there were created five spectacular two-storey Duplex Suites arranged across the aft end of Decks 9 and 10. Where it was once preferred for premium accommodations aboard steamships to be located amidships, in the quietest and most stable locations aboard, new trends revert once again to the ancient sailing ship preference of locating the Captain and Admiral's quarters at the stern, with large windows and often also with a private veranda. Celebrity's *Millennium* and Holland America's *Zuiderdam* were, at the time of the *QM2*'s planning, already being built with their top suites aft. While duplex layouts had been featured in two of the *QE2*'s veranda suites added during the seventies, and the P&O cruise ship *Aurora* featured two Mezzanine Suites, the *QM2* Duplexes would be of unprecedented size and luxury.

The *QM2*'s Duplexes each feature a double-height enclosed solarium with a wide curved stairway to its upper level, and with a spacious reception room, guest lavatory dining room and butler's pantry at their lower levels. The bedchamber above was accessed through wide sliding doors from a balcony along the solarium's inner side and provided with separate 'his' and 'hers' bathrooms and ample walk-in storage space further inboard. Again taking a cue from Eltham Palace, the bedchamber design was inspired by Virginia Courtauld's bedroom in the house, with its curved wall surfaces and circular indirect lighting feature above the bed. Where the room at Eltham was arranged to offer a view of the home's gardens from its bed, the *QM2* Duplexes feature a 'breakfast-in-bed' panorama through the solarium windows out over each suite's private terrace and to the sea beyond over the ship's afterdecks and stern. The view from these also recalled a similar outlook from the *Normandie*'s premiere Deauville and Trouville suites, situated as these were, on the curved aft quarters of the ship's sun deck above the café-grill restaurant.

An additional four single-level Royal Suites were arranged at the forward end of Deck 10 as a single-level adaptation of the Duplexes aft. These were in fact added at a fairly late stage of planning after plans fell through for a telecommunications and business centre that was to have occupied the same space.[24] Each of the four suites has a fully enclosed and furnished gallery with large windows overlooking the bow, and with the two outer suites also having open verandas at the ship's port and starboard sides as well as the unique shipboard feature of private access

*Seen here from the forward Deck 11 observation space, the bow deck features the same covered whaleback used in the **QE2** and the French Line **Normandie** of 1935. (Miles Cowsill)*

73

A study in curvilinear forms, the raked superstructure front is seen here with one of the spare azipod propeller blades kept on the ship's foredecks. (Miles Cowsill)

from the panoramic lifts tucked in behind the bridge wings. These suites can be combined into pairs or into a single super suite with a floor area of some 464.5 square metres occupying the entire forward end of Deck 10, with its own enclosed promenade around the curved superstructure front formed by opening connecting doors between their gallery spaces.

Although the *Queen Mary 2* was built beyond any shadow of doubt to be a true express North Atlantic liner as much as to also be a cruise ship capable of service in all latitudes and of trans-Pacific and other long ocean passages on voyages circumnavigating the globe, she differs from her predecessors in a number of significant details. Unlike the *Normandie* or old Cunard 'Queens', the *QM2* is able to sail in cruise service for considerably longer periods of time without needing to refuel and re-provision. She lacks the greater amount of below-decks space for 'hold' or 'not wanted during voyage' trunks and other heavy baggage once expected by passengers moving from one place to another by sea, though additional baggage rooms and storage space beneath the bow-deck whaleback is provided in the new ship. There was no repeat of the *QE2*'s garage with its side-loading hatches and car lift, as without the *QM2* being designed as a vehicle-carrying ship per se, current fire regulations would require the fuel tanks of all vehicles be drained prior to being taken aboard.[25] There are kennels for those taking their pets on transatlantic crossings. The new ship does carry the official RMS (Royal Mail Ship) designation, granted to Samuel Cunard's first *Britannia* and her original three sisters that made their North Atlantic debut as far back as 1840. While Cunard's ships are no longer a key carrier of the Royal Mail, the RMS (Royal Mail Ship) designation does provide for mail posted on board to be postmarked with the ship's name.

Unmistakably a descendant, first of the original slender QE2 stack, then its portlier version in Cunard colours after the re-engining, the Queen Mary 2 funnel height was circumscribed by the ship's need to pass beneath New York's Verrazano Narrows bridge. (Miles Cowsill)

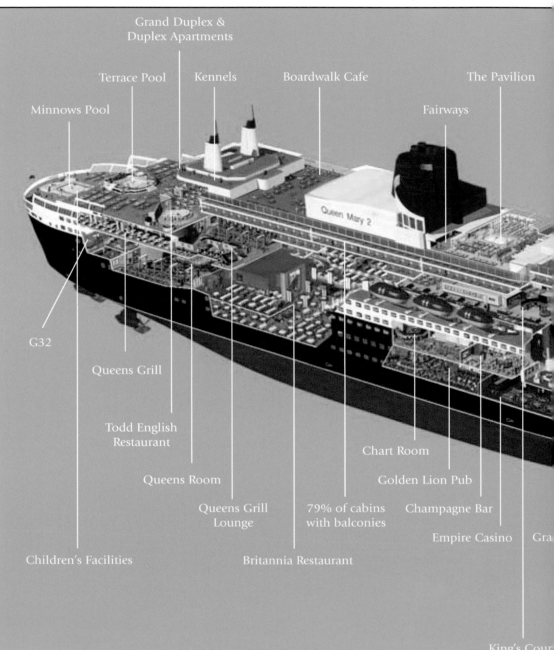

Grand Duplex &
Duplex Apartments

Terrace Pool   Kennels   Boardwalk Cafe   The Pavilion

Minnows Pool   Fairways

Queen Mary 2

G32

Queens Grill

Todd English
Restaurant

Chart Room

Queens Room   Golden Lion Pub

Queens Grill   79% of cabins   Champagne Bar
Lounge   with balconies

Empire Casino   Gra

Children's Facilities   Britannia Restaurant

King's Cour

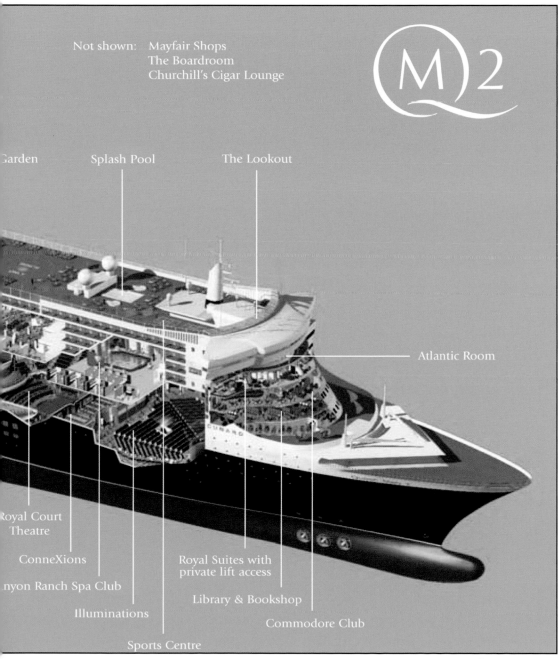

Not shown: Mayfair Shops
The Boardroom
Churchill's Cigar Lounge

MQ2

Garden

Splash Pool

The Lookout

Atlantic Room

Royal Court
Theatre

ConneXions

nyon Ranch Spa Club

Illuminations

Sports Centre

Royal Suites with
private lift access

Library & Bookshop

Commodore Club

CHAPTER 3

SOUTHAMPTON 2004

CUNARD

QUEEN MARY 2

The new *Queen Mary 2* was completed on schedule and officially handed over to Cunard on Monday 22nd December 2003. As the ship made an afternoon departure from the place of her birth, the people of Saint-Nazaire lined the Boulevard Albert 1er and Boulevard Présédent Wilson along the city's waterfront. Traffic on the Pont de Saint-Nazaire spanning the Loire Estuary came to a standstill, as it had done on 25th September when the ship left on her first sea trials, while motorists got out of their vehicles to watch the departure. For nearly four years, since Cunard and Chantiers had started working together in late 1999 and a temporary project site office was later opened at a circular building at Chantiers de l'Atlantique that was once the Yard restaurant, the *QM2* had in effect proudly belonged to, and been a key part of, Saint-Nazaire, the Pays de la Loire and indeed the whole of France.

Following the detailed planning stage, construction officially started on 16th January 2002 when Cunard's then President and CEO, Pamela Conover, pressed a button to set in motion the computer-controlled cutting of the ship's first steel plate. Nearly seven months later on 4th July an already fabricated 650-ton centre hull section was lowered into the yard's outer building dock, '*Forme B*', as it is known in French, in an official keel-laying ceremony. The honours were performed by the ship's designated Captain, Ronald Warwick, as a hand-held radio transceiver was handed to him by Pamela Conover and he spoke into it the words, "Crain driver, this is Captain Warwick speaking, please commence the building of my ship," signalling the lowering of hull blocks 502 and 503 precisely into position onto a grid of supporting blocks at the bottom of '*Forme B*'. The centre hull section was floated free of its supporting keel blocks for the first time in August and the nearly completed hull, with most of the superstructure also assembled was floated into

*Top & Above: The brand new **Queen Mary 2** makes her maiden arrival at her home port of Southampton on 26th December 2003. (Cunard)*

A head-on view of the Queen's Room's Hollywood bowl style bandstand, ahead of the room's hundred square metre parquet dance floor inlaid with a compass rose style pattern. (Cunard)

the deeper lower part of 'Forme B' on 1st December to make way for work to commence on the next ship, the Mediterranean Shipping Company's *MSC Opera*. On 16th March 2003 the *QM2* was towed some 400 metres downstream to 'Forme C' for completion and fitting-out.

'Forme C' is a large dry dock built initially as part of a Yard modernisation to handle supertanker work during the 1970s, and was in fact used for the construction of four gigantic *Batillus*-class ships, each with an overall length and beam of 414.2 and 63.01 metres respectively and a measure of 275,268 gross tons and deadweight tonnage of 555,000. The 'Forme Joubert' that also serves as a tidal lock accessing the Yard's inner 'Bassin de Penhoët' about half a kilometre further to the west was in fact built during the early 1930s to accommodate the *Normandie*, which was fitted out there. The 'Bassin de Penhoët' continues to be used as a fitting-out dock for passenger ships, at least those that fit through the 'Forme Joubert'. (The inclined launch ways where the *Normandie*'s hull was built and launched were located near the current location of 'Forme C'.) After completing her second sea trials, the *QM2*'s final drydocking was done in 'Forme C' alongside the fitting-out quay as her interiors and fitting-out were being completed.

As the brand new *QM2* set her bows towards the Bay of Biscay, showing on her starboard side a large banner with the words 'Merci Saint-Nazaire', there was a sense of loss and even great sadness among many of those that had gathered to bid farewell to a ship that for four years had been a significant part of their lives. There was the bitter-sweet feeling of saying goodbye to a young person who is leaving home to start his or her own life in the outside world that so many had experienced on the Clyde a generation earlier as the QE2 had made her way from Clydebank to Greenock when she departed her birthplace in November 1968.

On board the new *QM2* were many of those from Carnival

Top: The Band of the Royal Marines, Portsmouth during the **Queen Mary 2***'s naming ceremony in Southampton on 8th January 2004. (Cunard)*

Above: Carnival CEO Mickey Arison, Cunard Managing Director Pamela Conover, Captain Ronald Warwick and HM The Queen Elizabeth II pose for the media with the floodlit **Queen Mary 2** *at the ceremony's conclusion. (Cunard)*

and Cunard who had in effect lived in the Saint-Nazaire
vicinity for the foregoing four years and who were on their
way back eventually to their own homes in the Great Britain,
the United States and elsewhere. They, along with the ship's
officers and crew, the shipyard and supplier guarantee teams
and a number of invited guests celebrated Christmas on
board on what amounted to a pre-inaugural shakedown and
crew familiarisation voyage with a brief call at the Spanish
port of Vigo for manoeuvring and docking trials. As the ship
made her way up Southampton Water on Boxing Day, 26th
December, the first thing that struck all those who saw her
was her great size.

As Stephen Payne pointed out, there would be no need
for the *Queen Mary 2*'s size to be embellished or exaggerated
in paintings and other renderings done by marine artists, as
they did even with ships as large as the *Normandie* or the old
Cunard 'Queens'. She really was enormous enough to tower
above the foreground harbour tugs, sailing yachts and other
small craft shown in such art to glorify her prodigious scale.
The *QM2* uniquely conveyed the impression of a mighty
ocean liner by the more traditional balance of her hull and
superstructure proportions, which were approximately equal
rather than being dominated by the superstructure in the
style of most new cruise ships – and thanks to the longer
than now usual lengths of the bow and more gradually
terraced afterdecks.

At the time she was built, the *QM2* was the world's largest
passenger ship at a volumetric measure of 148,528 gross
tons, relegating Royal Caribbean's *Mariner of the Seas* to
second place at 138,279 tons. The *QM2*'s size has since been

*Left: The new **Queen Mary 2** meets up with her celebrated 1930s
predecessor **Queen Mary** at Long Beach, California on 23rd
February 2006 during a circumnavigation voyage around South
America. (Cunard)*

surpassed, first by the 154,407-ton *Freedom of the Seas* in 2006 and thence *Oasis of the Seas* in 2009 at a colossal supertanker size of 225,282 gross tons. The closest ship to the *QM2*'s size in the Carnival fleet at the time of writing was *Carnival Dream*, completed in 2009 at a measure of 128,251 tons. Yet the *QM2* continues to create a more impressive visual impression of greater stamina and strength than any of these, largely thanks to the more substantial massing and greater height of her North Atlantic hull. She also has the unique advantage of being a single one-of-a-kind ship built for a specific purpose rather then being one in a class- or series-building as are most of today's cruise ships. As such, the *QM2* already conveys the same 'aura of the singular' that was a hallmark of the *QE2* throughout her career until she was withdrawn from Cunard Line service in late 2008.

When Pamela Conover made various inspection tours of the ship at the Yard, she said that the thing that had struck her was the sheer size of the public rooms and the ceiling heights.[26] Where most modern cruise ships feature one or two high-ceilinged rooms extending through two or more decks, virtually all of the *QM2*'s public spaces on Decks 2 and 3 were given the added luxury of greater headroom typical of similarly large interiors in buildings. In fact, the *QM2* was perhaps the first ship since the *Normandie* to convey a true impression of building-like scale in her interiors.

Before starting her maiden voyage on 12th January 2004, the *QM2* spent 18 days alongside at the Port of Southampton's Queen Elizabeth II Terminal, a new facility named for the reigning monarch rather than the ship, replacing the Ocean Terminal that served the old Cunard 'Queens' since it opened in the early 1950s. During those days as the ship was made ready for sea with the loading of provisions and setting up the various services on board, she also hosted thousands of invited guests for luncheons, overnight stays and other functions from the media, travel

*This stern-quarter view of the **Queen Mary 2** docked in Southampton reveals the arrangement of windows in the dark charcoal-grey hull at various levels of the public rooms on the ship's lower decks. (Miles Cowsill)*

*The **Queen Mary 2** is given a fireboat welcome as she passes beneath the Golden Gate Bridge on her maiden call at San Francisco in 2004. (Cunard)*

industry and other people with various relationships to, and interests in, the ship and her owners. The highlight of this run-up to her debut was, of course the naming ceremony taken by Her Majesty the Queen Elizabeth II, herself naming for the second time a new Cunard 'Queen' following the *QE2* launching at Clydebank in September 1967, and having accompanied the late Queen Mother who launched the old *Queen Elizabeth* in 1938.

After a luncheon on board and a tour of the ship was made by Her Majesty and His Royal Highness Philip, The Duke of Edinburgh, the naming ceremony itself took place in a glass-walled temporary shelter erected next to the terminal for the event. In her opening welcome remarks and commentary, Cunard's Managing Director, Pamela Conover said:

"*Queen Mary 2* is a transatlantic liner with all the dignity and grace of the liners of the past. But she is also a transatlantic liner of the future with comforts and technology undreamt of when *Queen Elizabeth 2* was launched. Just as the original *Queen Mary* was the herald of an earlier golden age in ocean travel, so this ship heralds the new golden age; she represents no less than the triumph of a great tradition, a great British tradition of which we can all be proud."

Following this, came a stirring rendition of 'Amazing Grace' introduced solo on the bagpipes by the Queen's personal court piper, Lesley Garrett, and picked up as the tune progressed by the band of the Royal Marines. Her Majesty then stepped to the podium and spoke the time-honoured words, "I name this ship *Queen Mary 2*. May God bless her and all who sail in her." As the magnum of Veuve Clicquot anointed the starboard bow shell plating, the Cunard Line officially could claim to have two transatlantic 'Queens' for the first time since September 1967 when the old *Queen Mary* and *Queen Elizabeth* had saluted one another as they passed in opposite directions on their regular weekly

Top: With finishing touches such as the banding to be painted around of her forward windows, lifeboats and launches yet to be added and interior finishing completed, the ship runs her second sea trials. (Author's collection)

Above: The completed **Queen Mary 2** *on her arrival at Southampton. (Andrew Cooke)*

*An impressive aerial view of the **Queen Mary 2** underway at dusk, clearly showing her more traditional arrangement of longer than now usual expanse of terraced afterdecks. (Cunard)*

service for the last time before the *Queen Elizabeth* was
withdrawn from service. Although there would be no revival
of the weekly crossings with the *QE2* and the *QM2*, the two
ships would make their first of several tandem North Atlantic
crossings in April 2004 as part of the *QM2*'s maiden crossing
to New York. By then it had already been announced that a
third ship, *Queen Victoria* would be introduced the following
year, though this would be a slightly smaller ship derived
from the Holland American Vista series and intended
primarily for cruising with the added structural fortitude to
make occasional Atlantic crossings and other long sea
passages. This was ultimately postponed until late 2007 so
that service experience could be gained from the *QM2* and
the size of the new ship increased accordingly.

The excitement and great flurry of activity surrounding
the *QM2* during her naming and inauguration in her home
port of Southampton also included other events such as
Captain Ronald Warwick's promotion to Commodore,
following in the footsteps of his father, William Warwick, who
had been the *QE2*'s designated Master during her building
and through her first years of service. The 'Blue Peter'
people from BBC Television also caught up with Stephen
Payne, arranging for him to give them a tour of the ship that
was filmed for the programme. This opportunity was taken
also to present him with a gold 'Blue Peter' badge, the
organisation's highest honour for outstanding achievement.
Although Stephen received an OBE (Order of the British
Empire) the following year honouring him for his "services
to the shipping industry" the following year, and was elected
as the President of the Royal Institution of Naval Architects
in 2006, the 'Blue Peter' gold badge was for him personally a
particularly special honour – he respectfully points out that
the 'Blue Peter' gold badge is in fact rarer than the OBE,
and that he is probably the oldest person ever to have
received one.

Top: Only four years after her debut, the **Queen Mary 2** *was joined by her albeit smaller, though nonetheless 'Queen'-class, fleet mate* **Queen Victoria** *seen here at Southampton. (Miles Cowsill)*

Above: The new **Queen Elizabeth**, *the current Cunard fleet's third 'Queen'-class ship seen here at her home port of Southampton shortly after her completion. (Andrew Cooke)*

After having designed more than 30 ships – he lost count some time ago – Stephen has never forgotten his childhood visit to Southampton and the then brand new *QE2* all those years ago. As the most significant ship he has thus far designed, he has followed the *QM2* through her service life, taking the time on the occasion of her fifth anniversary in 2009 to send greetings to many of the key people he had worked with through 'Project Queen Mary' and the ship's actual building and commissioning. By then 'his ship' had already sailed 750,000 nautical miles and had made 104 North Atlantic crossings.

Stephen Payne has also become a popular figure, giving illustrated talks on ships and shipping history when he travels aboard the *QM2* and through his appearances on various television features dealing with ships and engineering subjects of general public interest. He has become an inspiration and mentor to other young people seeking careers in engineering, naval architecture and other technical specialties who are facing the same obstacles from which he was kindly rescued by Justin Johnson – one young lady aspiring to study engineering told him in a letter that her school had advised her that she should seek something more feminine as her career.

He has set up the Future Engineers programme with its own website, and with the support of Cunard, an arrangement for young people interested in an engineering career to be given the rare opportunity to visit the *Queen Mary 2* as a source of inspiration to them in the same way that the *QE2* and 'Blue Peter' had inspired him – and yes, young people today still dream of creating wonderful new ships, as illustrated on the Line's 'We are Cunard' Internet blog that showed a rendering of a futuristic aft-engined Cunarder submitted by 13-year-old Jasper Rönnebrand from Sweden. This can surely be an inspiration to all of us.

*A bow quarter-view of the **Queen Mary 2** at Southampton, giving a compelling impression of the ship's great size and structural strength. (Miles Cowsill)*

*The **Queen Mary 2** alongside the Pier Head landing stage on 20th October 2009 in Liverpool, the place of Cunard's birth, with the three graces, the Royal Liver Building, the old Cunard head office and domed Mersey Docks and Harbour Board building in the background.*

(Cunard)

REFERENCES

1 Stephen Payne, 'History re-written' *Queen Mary 2: Genesis of a Queen*, RINA, London, p. 71

2 *The Shipping World*, 7th February 1962, p. 171

3 *Shipbuilding and Shipping Record*, London, 31st January, 1969

4 Michael Kenward, "Shipbuilder Extraordinaire," *Ingena*, December 2009, p. 51

5 Brian Lusk, "By air over the North Atlantic," *Airways*, May/June 1997, p. 26

6 *The Motor Ship*, July 1965, p. 146-7

7 Neil Potter & Jack Frost, *Queen Elizabeth 2: The authorised story*, p. 141

8 Bruce Peter, Philip Dawson, Ian Johnston, *QE2: Britain's greatest liner*, p. 61

9 Bruce Peter, *Knud E. Hansen A/S: Ship design through seven decades*, p. 202-3

10 Sir Hugh Casson, *The Times*, Special QE2 Supplement, Tuesday 29th April, 1969

11 "Drawing up an efficient design," *The Naval Architect*, QM2 souvenir edition, p. 19

12 Mickey Arison, "Cunard's line of succession," *Lloyd's Cruise International*, QM2 souvenir edition, December 2001, p. 9

13 Cunard media release, June 1998

14 Gerry Ellis, "Creating a new Atlantic liner," *The Naval Architect*, QM2 souvenir edition, p. 7

15 "Drawing up an efficient design," *The Naval Architect*, QM2 souvenir edition, p. 20

16 "Drawing up an efficient design," *The Naval Architect*, QM2 souvenir edition, p. 21

17 Michael Kenward, "Shipbuilder Extraordinaire," *Ingena*, December 2009, p. 53

18 Author discussion with John Maxtone-Graham, New York, 9th February 2004

19 Philip Dawson, "Design trend report," *ShipPax Designs 2000*

20 Author discussion with Tomas Tillberg, Fort Lauderdale, 5th June 2001

21 Author discussion with Andy Collier of SMC Design in London, 11th May 2001

22 Author discussion with Frederik Johansson of Tillberg Design at shipyard, 26th November 2003

23 Author discussion with Stephen Payne, 15th August 2002

24 Philip Dawson, "Hail to the new Queen," *ShipPax Designs 04*, p. 76

25 Author discussion with Stephen Payne, 15th August 2002

26 "The woman behind the Queen," *Lloyd's Cruise International*, QM2 souvenir edition, December 2001, p. 11

POSTSCRIPT

Justin Johnson died from prostate cancer just a few months before the *Queen Mary 2* was completed. In honour of Justin and in recognition of the role he played in my life, I placed an obituary dedicated to his memory behind one of the panels of the ship whilst she was completing. My hope is that this will be discovered when the ship is finally broken up. It describes that the *Queen Mary 2* would not have taken the form that she did if Justin had not convinced me to stick to my guns and become a naval architect against official school advice.

Stephen Payne, March 2011

QUEEN MARY 2
CUNARD LINE,
SOUTHAMPTON

Builders: *Chantiers de l'Atlantique, Saint-Nazaire, France*

Keel laid: 4 July 2001

Floated out: 1 December 2002

Delivered: 22 December 2003

Yard number: G32

IMO number: 9241061

Flag: United Kingdom

Port of registry: Southampton

Classification: Lloyd's Register +100A1

Overall dimensions

Length overall: 345.03 m

Waterline length: 301.35 m

Beam: 41.00 m

Draft: 10.30 m

Air draft (Height above waterline): 62.00 m

Depth to bulkhead deck (Deck 1): 13.70 m

Depth to Promenade Deck (Deck 7): 23.94 m

Measure and capacities

Gross tonnage (GT): 148,258

Net tonnage (NT): 98,720

Deadweight tonnage (tDW): 19,189

Passengers, lower berths: 2,620

Passengers, maximum: 3,090 including fold-away upper berths and settee beds

Passenger accommodations: 1,310 cabins and suites, 73% with outside exposure, 71% with private verandas

Officers, crew and staff: 1,238

Fuel capacity: 5,300 m2

Fresh water capacity: 3,700 m2

Machinery and performance

Power: CODAG (Combined diesel and gas-turbine), 3 diesel generator sets and two aviation-style gas turbine generators in total generating 120 mW of electrical power.

Propulsion: 4 external propeller pods, 2 azimuthing, 2 fixed yielding a total motive power of 86 mW

Trial speed: 29.63 knots

Service speed: 26.5 knots

Manoeuvring: 3 transverse bow thrusters used in conjunction with the pods for docking

Stabilisation: 4 retractable anti-rolling fins

*A mood impression of the **Queen Mary 2** passing the Nab Tower that stands at the deep water entrance to the Solent and to her home port of Southampton. (Robert Lloyd)*

ACKNOWLEDGEMENTS

Once again, my sincere thanks to Miles and Linda Cowsill of Lily Publications for giving me the opportunity to tell this story and share some of my thoughts and personal impressions associated with the Cunard Line and the *Queen Mary 2*. I am also especially grateful to Stephen Payne for sharing his own story and images with us and for his review of the text for the fidelity of its technical content, as well as to the people at Carnival Corporation, Cunard Line, Chantiers de l'Atlantique and Tillberg Design without whose whole-hearted collaboration this work would never have been entirely possible. Our thanks also go to Clare Price and Nicola Green for their production support at Lily Publications and to Caroline Hallworth for her careful editing and proofing of the text, to Gomer Press for their printing and binding of the book and to Rebecca Money of Ocean Books for her continuing support and enthusiasm. We also thank Michael Gallagher for his continuing help with images and other material from Cunard's resources and his continuing overall support of our publishing endeavours.

The story also draws upon interviews and other material I obtained at the time of the *Queen Mary 2*'s design, building and commissioning, for which I once again express my gratitude to, Eric Chapuis, Jean-Jacques Gatepaille, Chantiers de l'Atlantique; Pamela Conover, Gerry Ellis, Cunard Line; Eric Mouzourides, designteam; Andy Collier, Andy Yuill, SMC Design, Robert and Tomas Tillberg, Frederik Johansson, Anders Lund-Rasmussen, Tillberg Design, Morten Matheisen, John Maxtone-Graham and Robert Lloyd.

Thanks also goes to Andrew Cooke, John Hendy, Bruce Peter and FotoFlite for their assistance with photographs for the book.